CAMBRIDGE

IELTS
ACADEMIC 15

WITH ANSWERS

AUTHENTIC PRACTICE TESTS

Cambridge University Press
www.cambridge.org/elt

Cambridge Assessment English
www.cambridgeenglish.org

Information on this title: www.cambridge.org/9781108781619

© Cambridge University Press and Cambridge Assessment 2020

It is normally necessary for written permission for copying to be obtained
in advance from a publisher. The sample answer sheets at the back of this
book are designed to be copied and distributed in class.

The normal requirements are waived here and it is not necessary to write to
Cambridge University Press for permission for an individual teacher to make copies
for use within his or her own classroom. Only those pages that carry the wording
'© Cambridge Assessment 2020 Photocopiable ' may be copied.

First published 2020

20 19 18 17 16 15 14 13 12 11 10 9 8 7 6 5 4 3 2 1

Printed in Malaysia by Vivar Printing

A catalogue record for this publication is available from the British Library

ISBN 978-1-108-78161-9 Academic Student's Book with Answers with Audio
ISBN 978-1-108-78162-6 General Training Student's Book with Answers with Audio

The publishers have no responsibility for the persistence or accuracy of URLs
for external or third-party internet websites referred to in this publication, and
do not guarantee that any content on such websites is, or will remain, accurate
or appropriate. Information regarding prices, travel timetables, and other factual
information given in this work is correct at the time of first printing but the
publishers do not guarantee the accuracy of such information thereafter.

Contents

Introduction

Prepare for the exam with practice tests from Cambridge

Inside you'll find four authentic examination papers from Cambridge Assessment English. They are the perfect way to practise – EXACTLY like the real exam.

Why are they unique?

All our authentic practice tests go through the same design process as the IELTS test. We check every single part of our practice tests with real students under exam conditions, to make sure we give you the most authentic experience possible.

Students can practise these tests on their own or with the help of a teacher to familiarise themselves with the exam format, understand the scoring system and practise exam technique.

Further information

IELTS is jointly managed by the British Council, IDP: IELTS Australia and Cambridge Assessment English. Further information can be found on the IELTS official website at: **ielts.org**.

WHAT IS THE TEST FORMAT?

IELTS consists of four components. All candidates take the same Listening and Speaking tests. There is a choice of Reading and Writing tests according to whether a candidate is taking the Academic or General Training module.

Academic	General Training
For candidates wishing to study at undergraduate or postgraduate levels, and for those seeking professional registration.	For candidates wishing to migrate to an English-speaking country (Australia, Canada, New Zealand, UK), and for those wishing to train or study below degree level.

The test components are taken in the following order:

Listening 4 parts, 40 items, approximately 30 minutes		
Academic Reading 3 sections, 40 items 60 minutes	or	**General Training Reading** 3 sections, 40 items 60 minutes
Academic Writing 2 tasks 60 minutes	or	**General Training Writing** 2 tasks 60 minutes
Speaking 11 to 14 minutes		
Total Test Time 2 hours 44 minutes		

ACADEMIC TEST FORMAT

Listening

This test consists of four parts, each with ten questions. The first two parts are concerned with social needs. The first part is a conversation between two speakers and the second part is a monologue. The final two parts are concerned with situations related to educational or training contexts. The third part is a conversation between up to four people and the fourth part is a monologue.

A variety of question types is used, including: multiple choice, matching, plan/map/ diagram labelling, form completion, note completion, table completion, flow-chart completion, summary completion, sentence completion and short-answer questions.

Candidates hear the recording once only and answer the questions as they listen. Ten minutes are allowed at the end for candidates to transfer their answers to the answer sheet.

Reading

This test consists of three sections with 40 questions. There are three texts, which are taken from journals, books, magazines and newspapers. The texts are on topics of general interest. At least one text contains detailed logical argument.

A variety of question types is used, including: multiple choice, identifying information (True/False/Not Given), identifying the writer's views/claims (Yes/No/Not Given), matching information, matching headings, matching features, matching sentence endings, sentence completion, summary completion, note completion, table completion, flow-chart completion, diagram-label completion and short-answer questions.

Writing

This test consists of two tasks. It is suggested that candidates spend about 20 minutes on Task 1, which requires them to write at least 150 words, and 40 minutes on Task 2, which requires them to write at least 250 words. Task 2 contributes twice as much as Task 1 to the Writing score.

Task 1 requires candidates to look at a diagram or some data (in a graph, table or chart) and to present the information in their own words. They are assessed on their ability to organise, present and possibly compare data, and are required to describe the stages of a process, describe an object or event, or explain how something works.

In Task 2, candidates are presented with a point of view, argument or problem. They are assessed on their ability to present a solution to the problem, present and justify an opinion, compare and contrast evidence and opinions, and to evaluate and challenge ideas, evidence or arguments.

Candidates are also assessed on their ability to write in an appropriate style. More information on assessing the Writing test, including Writing assessment criteria (public version), is available at ielts.org.

Speaking

This test takes between 11 and 14 minutes and is conducted by a trained examiner. There are three parts:

Part 1

The candidate and the examiner introduce themselves. Candidates then answer general questions about themselves, their home/family, their job/studies, their interests and a wide range of similar familiar topic areas. This part lasts between four and five minutes.

Part 2

The candidate is given a task card with prompts and is asked to talk on a particular topic. The candidate has one minute to prepare and they can make some notes if they wish, before speaking for between one and two minutes. The examiner then asks one or two questions on the same topic.

Part 3

The examiner and the candidate engage in a discussion of more abstract issues which are thematically linked to the topic in Part 2. The discussion lasts between four and five minutes.

The Speaking test assesses whether candidates can communicate effectively in English. The assessment takes into account Fluency and Coherence, Lexical Resource, Grammatical Range and Accuracy, and Pronunciation. More information on assessing the Speaking test, including Speaking assessment criteria (public version), is available at ielts.org.

HOW IS IELTS SCORED?

IELTS results are reported on a nine-band scale. In addition to the score for overall language ability, IELTS provides a score in the form of a profile for each of the four skills (Listening, Reading, Writing and Speaking). These scores are also reported on a nine-band scale. All scores are recorded on the Test Report Form along with details of the candidate's nationality, first language and date of birth. Each Overall Band Score corresponds to a descriptive statement which gives a summary of the English-language ability of a candidate classified at that level. The nine bands and their descriptive statements are as follows:

9   ***Expert User*** – *Has fully operational command of the language: appropriate, accurate and fluent with complete understanding.*

8   ***Very Good User*** – *Has fully operational command of the language with only occasional unsystematic inaccuracies and inappropriacies. Misunderstandings may occur in unfamiliar situations. Handles complex detailed argumentation well.*

7   ***Good User*** – *Has operational command of the language, though with occasional inaccuracies, inappropriacies and misunderstandings in some situations. Generally handles complex language well and understands detailed reasoning.*

6   ***Competent User*** – *Has generally effective command of the language despite some inaccuracies, inappropriacies and misunderstandings. Can use and understand fairly complex language, particularly in familiar situations.*

5   ***Modest User*** – *Has partial command of the language, coping with overall meaning in most situations, though is likely to make many mistakes. Should be able to handle basic communication in own field.*

4   ***Limited User*** – *Basic competence is limited to familiar situations. Has frequent problems in understanding and expression. Is not able to use complex language.*

3   ***Extremely Limited User*** – *Conveys and understands only general meaning in very familiar situations. Frequent breakdowns in communication occur.*

2   ***Intermittent User*** – *No real communication is possible except for the most basic information using isolated words or short formulae in familiar situations and to meet immediate needs. Has great difficulty understanding spoken and written English.*

1   ***Non User*** – *Essentially has no ability to use the language beyond possibly a few isolated words.*

0   ***Did not attempt the test*** – *No assessable information provided.*

MARKING THE PRACTICE TESTS

Listening and Reading

The answer keys are on pages 119–126.
Each question in the Listening and Reading tests is worth one mark.

Questions which require letter / Roman numeral answers

- For questions where the answers are letters or Roman numerals, you should write *only* the number of answers required. For example, if the answer is a single letter or numeral you should write only one answer. If you have written more letters or numerals than are required, the answer must be marked wrong.

Questions which require answers in the form of words or numbers

- Answers may be written in upper or lower case.
- Words in brackets are *optional* – they are correct, but not necessary.
- Alternative answers are separated by a slash (/).
- If you are asked to write an answer using a certain number of words and/or (a) number(s), you will be penalised if you exceed this. For example, if a question specifies an answer using NO MORE THAN THREE WORDS and the correct answer is 'black leather coat', the answer 'coat of black leather' is *incorrect*.
- In questions where you are expected to complete a gap, you should only transfer the necessary missing word(s) onto the answer sheet. For example, to complete 'in the …', where the correct answer is 'morning', the answer 'in the morning' would be *incorrect*.
- All answers require correct spelling (including words in brackets).
- Both US and UK spelling are acceptable and are included in the answer key.
- All standard alternatives for numbers, dates and currencies are acceptable.
- All standard abbreviations are acceptable.
- You will find additional notes about individual answers in the answer key.

Writing

The sample answers are on pages 127–137. It is not possible for you to give yourself a mark for the Writing tasks. We have provided sample answers (written by candidates), showing their score and the examiners' comments. These sample answers will give you an insight into what is required for the Writing test.

HOW SHOULD YOU INTERPRET YOUR SCORES?

At the end of each Listening and Reading answer key you will find a chart which will help you assess whether, on the basis of your Practice Test results, you are ready to take the IELTS test.

In interpreting your score, there are a number of points you should bear in mind. Your performance in the real IELTS test will be reported in two ways: there will be a Band Score from 1 to 9 for each of the components and an Overall Band Score from 1 to 9, which is the average of your scores in the four components. However, institutions considering your application are advised to look at both the Overall Band Score and the Band Score for each component in order to determine whether you have the language skills needed for a particular course of study. For example, if your course involves a lot of reading and writing, but no lectures, listening skills might be less important and a score of 5 in Listening might be acceptable if the Overall Band Score was 7. However, for a course which has lots of lectures and spoken instructions, a score of 5 in Listening might be unacceptable even though the Overall Band Score was 7.

Once you have marked your tests, you should have some idea of whether your listening and reading skills are good enough for you to try the IELTS test. If you did well enough in one component, but not in others, you will have to decide for yourself whether you are ready to take the test.

The Practice Tests have been checked to ensure that they are the same level of difficulty as the real IELTS test. However, we cannot guarantee that your score in the Practice Tests will be reflected in the real IELTS test. The Practice Tests can only give you an idea of your possible future performance and it is ultimately up to you to make decisions based on your score.

Different institutions accept different IELTS scores for different types of courses. We have based our recommendations on the average scores which the majority of institutions accept. The institution to which you are applying may, of course, require a higher or lower score than most other institutions.

Test 1

PART 1   *Questions 1–10*

Complete the notes below.

*Write **ONE WORD AND/OR A NUMBER** for each answer.*

Listening test audio

Bankside Recruitment Agency

- Address of agency: 497 Eastside, Docklands
- Name of agent: Becky **1** ....
- Phone number: 07866 510333
- Best to call her in the **2** ....

Typical jobs

- Clerical and admin roles, mainly in the finance industry
- Must have good **3** .... skills
- Jobs are usually for at least one **4** ....
- Pay is usually **5** £ .... per hour

Registration process

- Wear a **6** .... to the interview
- Must bring your **7** .... to the interview
- They will ask questions about each applicant's **8** ....

Advantages of using an agency

- The **9** .... you receive at interview will benefit you
- Will get access to vacancies which are not advertised
- Less **10** .... is involved in applying for jobs

PART 2   *Questions 11–20*

Questions 11–14

*Choose the correct letter, **A**, **B** or **C**.*

Listening test audio

Matthews Island Holidays

11 According to the speaker, the company

   A   has been in business for longer than most of its competitors.
   B   arranges holidays to more destinations than its competitors.
   C   has more customers than its competitors.

12 Where can customers meet the tour manager before travelling to the Isle of Man?

   A   Liverpool
   B   Heysham
   C   Luton

13 How many lunches are included in the price of the holiday?

   A   three
   B   four
   C   five

14 Customers have to pay extra for

   A   guaranteeing themselves a larger room.
   B   booking at short notice.
   C   transferring to another date.

Questions 15–20

Complete the table below.

*Write **ONE WORD AND/OR A NUMBER** for each answer.*

Timetable for Isle of Man holiday		
	Activity	**Notes**
Day 1	Arrive	Introduction by manager Hotel dining room has view of the **15** ....
Day 2	Tynwald Exhibition and Peel	Tynwald may have been founded in **16** .... not 979.
Day 3	Trip to Snaefell	Travel along promenade in a tram; train to Laxey; train to the **17** .... of Snaefell
Day 4	Free day	Company provides a **18** .... for local transport and heritage sites.
Day 5	Take the **19** .... railway train from Douglas to Port Erin	Free time, then coach to Castletown – former **20** .... has old castle.
Day 6	Leave	Leave the island by ferry or plane

PART 3   *Questions 21–30*

Questions 21–26

What did findings of previous research claim about the personality traits a child is likely to have because of their position in the family?

Listening test audio

*Choose **SIX** answers from the box and write the correct letter, **A–H**, next to Questions 21–26.*

Personality Traits
A   outgoing
B   selfish
C   independent
D   attention-seeking
E   introverted
F   co-operative
G   caring
H   competitive

Position in family

21   the eldest child   ....

22   a middle child   ....

23   the youngest child   ....

24   a twin   ....

25   an only child   ....

26   a child with much older siblings   ....

Questions 27 and 28

*Choose the correct letter, **A**, **B** or **C**.*

27 What do the speakers say about the evidence relating to birth order and academic success?

    A   There is conflicting evidence about whether oldest children perform best in intelligence tests.

    B   There is little doubt that birth order has less influence on academic achievement than socio-economic status.

    C   Some studies have neglected to include important factors such as family size.

28 What does Ruth think is surprising about the difference in oldest children's academic performance?

    A   It is mainly thanks to their roles as teachers for their younger siblings.

    B   The advantages they have only lead to a slightly higher level of achievement.

    C   The extra parental attention they receive at a young age makes little difference.

Questions 29 and 30

*Choose **TWO** letters, **A–E**.*

Which **TWO** experiences of sibling rivalry do the speakers agree has been valuable for them?

    A   learning to share

    B   learning to stand up for oneself

    C   learning to be a good loser

    D   learning to be tolerant

    E   learning to say sorry

PART 4   *Questions 31–40*

Complete the notes below.

*Write **ONE WORD ONLY** for each answer.*

Listening test audio

The Eucalyptus Tree in Australia

Importance

- it provides **31** .... and food for a wide range of species
- its leaves provide **32** .... which is used to make a disinfectant

Reasons for present decline in number

A) Diseases

(i) 'Mundulla Yellows'

- Cause – lime used for making **33** .... was absorbed
  - trees were unable to take in necessary iron through their roots

(ii) 'Bell-miner Associated Die-back'

- Cause – **34** .... feed on eucalyptus leaves
  - they secrete a substance containing sugar
  - bell-miner birds are attracted by this and keep away other species

B) Bushfires

William Jackson's theory:

- high-frequency bushfires have impact on vegetation, resulting in the growth of **35** ....
- mid-frequency bushfires result in the growth of eucalyptus forests, because they:
  - make more **36** .... available to the trees
  - maintain the quality of the **37** ....
- low-frequency bushfires result in the growth of **38** '................................... rainforest', which is:
  - a **39** .... ecosystem
  - an ideal environment for the **40** .... of the bell-miner

---

→ 🔊 p. 119 📄 p. 99 15

READING

READING PASSAGE 1

*You should spend about 20 minutes on **Questions 1–13**, which are based on Reading Passage 1 below.*

Nutmeg – a valuable spice

The nutmeg tree, *Myristica fragrans*, is a large evergreen tree native to Southeast Asia. Until the late 18th century, it only grew in one place in the world: a small group of islands in the Banda Sea, part of the Moluccas – or Spice Islands – in northeastern Indonesia. The tree is thickly branched with dense foliage of tough, dark green oval leaves, and produces small, yellow, bell-shaped flowers and pale yellow pear-shaped fruits. The fruit is encased in a fleshy husk. When the fruit is ripe, this husk splits into two halves along a ridge running the length of the fruit. Inside is a purple-brown shiny seed, 2–3 cm long by about 2 cm across, surrounded by a lacy red or crimson covering called an 'aril'. These are the sources of the two spices nutmeg and mace, the former being produced from the dried seed and the latter from the aril.

Nutmeg was a highly prized and costly ingredient in European cuisine in the Middle Ages, and was used as a flavouring, medicinal, and preservative agent. Throughout this period, the Arabs were the exclusive importers of the spice to Europe. They sold nutmeg for high prices to merchants based in Venice, but they never revealed the exact location of the source of this extremely valuable commodity. The Arab-Venetian dominance of the trade finally ended in 1512, when the Portuguese reached the Banda Islands and began exploiting its precious resources.

Always in danger of competition from neighbouring Spain, the Portuguese began subcontracting their spice distribution to Dutch traders. Profits began to flow into the Netherlands, and the Dutch commercial fleet swiftly grew into one of the largest in the world. The Dutch quietly gained control of most of the shipping and trading of spices in Northern Europe. Then, in 1580, Portugal fell under Spanish rule, and by the end of the 16th century the Dutch found themselves locked out of the market. As prices for pepper, nutmeg, and other spices soared across Europe, they decided to fight back.

In 1602, Dutch merchants founded the VOC, a trading corporation better known as the Dutch East India Company. By 1617, the VOC was the richest commercial operation in the world. The company had 50,000 employees worldwide, with a private army of 30,000 men and a fleet of 200 ships. At the same time, thousands of people across Europe were dying of the plague, a highly contagious and deadly disease. Doctors were desperate for a way to stop the spread of this disease, and they decided nutmeg held the cure. Everybody wanted nutmeg, and many were willing to spare no expense to have it. Nutmeg bought for a few pennies in Indonesia could be sold for 68,000 times its original cost on the streets of London. The only problem was the short supply. And that's where the Dutch found their opportunity.

The Banda Islands were ruled by local sultans who insisted on maintaining a neutral trading policy towards foreign powers. This allowed them to avoid the presence of Portuguese or Spanish troops on their soil, but it also left them unprotected from other invaders. In 1621, the Dutch arrived and took over. Once securely in control of the Bandas, the Dutch went to work protecting their new investment. They concentrated all nutmeg production into a few easily guarded areas, uprooting and destroying any trees outside the plantation zones. Anyone caught growing a nutmeg seedling or carrying seeds without the proper authority was severely punished. In addition, all exported nutmeg was covered with lime to make sure there was no chance a fertile seed which could be grown elsewhere would leave the islands. There was only one obstacle to Dutch domination. One of the Banda Islands, a sliver of land called Run, only 3 km long by less than 1 km wide, was under the control of the British. After decades of fighting for control of this tiny island, the Dutch and British arrived at a compromise settlement, the Treaty of Breda, in 1667. Intent on securing their hold over every nutmeg-producing island, the Dutch offered a trade: if the British would give them the island of Run, they would in turn give Britain a distant and much less valuable island in North America. The British agreed. That other island was Manhattan, which is how New Amsterdam became New York. The Dutch now had a monopoly over the nutmeg trade which would last for another century.

Then, in 1770, a Frenchman named Pierre Poivre successfully smuggled nutmeg plants to safety in Mauritius, an island off the coast of Africa. Some of these were later exported to the Caribbean where they thrived, especially on the island of Grenada. Next, in 1778, a volcanic eruption in the Banda region caused a tsunami that wiped out half the nutmeg groves. Finally, in 1809, the British returned to Indonesia and seized the Banda Islands by force. They returned the islands to the Dutch in 1817, but not before transplanting hundreds of nutmeg seedlings to plantations in several locations across southern Asia. The Dutch nutmeg monopoly was over.

Today, nutmeg is grown in Indonesia, the Caribbean, India, Malaysia, Papua New Guinea and Sri Lanka, and world nutmeg production is estimated to average between 10,000 and 12,000 tonnes per year.

Questions 1–4

Complete the notes below.

*Choose **ONE WORD ONLY** from the passage for each answer.*

Write your answers in boxes 1–4 on your answer sheet.

The nutmeg tree and fruit

- the leaves of the tree are **1** .... in shape

- the **2** .... surrounds the fruit and breaks open when the fruit is ripe

- the **3** .... is used to produce the spice nutmeg

- the covering known as the aril is used to produce **4** ....

- the tree has yellow flowers and fruit

Questions 5–7

Do the following statements agree with the information given in Reading Passage 1?

In boxes 5–7 on your answer sheet, write

TRUE	*if the statement agrees with the information*
FALSE	*if the statement contradicts the information*
NOT GIVEN	*if there is no information on this*

5 In the Middle Ages, most Europeans knew where nutmeg was grown.

6 The VOC was the world's first major trading company.

7 Following the Treaty of Breda, the Dutch had control of all the islands where nutmeg grew.

Questions 8–13

Complete the table below.

Choose **ONE WORD ONLY** *from the passage for each answer.*

Write your answers in boxes 8–13 on your answer sheet.

Middle Ages	Nutmeg was brought to Europe by the **8** ....
16th century	European nations took control of the nutmeg trade
17th century	Demand for nutmeg grew, as it was believed to be effective against the disease known as the **9** .... The Dutch – took control of the Banda Islands – restricted nutmeg production to a few areas – put **10** .... on nutmeg to avoid it being cultivated outside the islands – finally obtained the island of **11** .... from the British
Late 18th century	1770 – nutmeg plants were secretly taken to **12** .... 1778 – half the Banda Islands' nutmeg plantations were destroyed by a **13** ....

→  p. 120   19

READING PASSAGE 2

You should spend about 20 minutes on **Questions 14–26**, *which are based on Reading Passage 2 below.*

Driverless cars

A   The automotive sector is well used to adapting to automation in manufacturing. The implementation of robotic car manufacture from the 1970s onwards led to significant cost savings and improvements in the reliability and flexibility of vehicle mass production. A new challenge to vehicle production is now on the horizon and, again, it comes from automation. However, this time it is not to do with the manufacturing process, but with the vehicles themselves.

    Research projects on vehicle automation are not new. Vehicles with limited self-driving capabilities have been around for more than 50 years, resulting in significant contributions towards driver assistance systems. But since Google announced in 2010 that it had been trialling self-driving cars on the streets of California, progress in this field has quickly gathered pace.

B   There are many reasons why technology is advancing so fast. One frequently cited motive is safety; indeed, research at the UK's Transport Research Laboratory has demonstrated that more than 90 percent of road collisions involve human error as a contributory factor, and it is the primary cause in the vast majority. Automation may help to reduce the incidence of this.

    Another aim is to free the time people spend driving for other purposes. If the vehicle can do some or all of the driving, it may be possible to be productive, to socialise or simply to relax while automation systems have responsibility for safe control of the vehicle. If the vehicle can do the driving, those who are challenged by existing mobility models – such as older or disabled travellers – may be able to enjoy significantly greater travel autonomy.

C   Beyond these direct benefits, we can consider the wider implications for transport and society, and how manufacturing processes might need to respond as a result. At present, the average car spends more than 90 percent of its life parked. Automation means that initiatives for car-sharing become much more viable, particularly in urban areas with significant travel demand. If a significant proportion of the population choose to use shared automated vehicles, mobility demand can be met by far fewer vehicles.

D   The Massachusetts Institute of Technology investigated automated mobility in Singapore, finding that fewer than 30 percent of the vehicles currently used would be required if fully automated car sharing could be implemented. If this is the case, it might mean that we need to manufacture far fewer vehicles to meet demand.

However, the number of trips being taken would probably increase, partly because empty vehicles would have to be moved from one customer to the next.

Modelling work by the University of Michigan Transportation Research Institute suggests automated vehicles might reduce vehicle ownership by 43 percent, but that vehicles' average annual mileage would double as a result. As a consequence, each vehicle would be used more intensively, and might need replacing sooner. This faster rate of turnover may mean that vehicle production will not necessarily decrease.

E   Automation may prompt other changes in vehicle manufacture. If we move to a model where consumers are tending not to own a single vehicle but to purchase access to a range of vehicles through a mobility provider, drivers will have the freedom to select one that best suits their needs for a particular journey, rather than making a compromise across all their requirements.

Since, for most of the time, most of the seats in most cars are unoccupied, this may boost production of a smaller, more efficient range of vehicles that suit the needs of individuals. Specialised vehicles may then be available for exceptional journeys, such as going on a family camping trip or helping a son or daughter move to university.

F   There are a number of hurdles to overcome in delivering automated vehicles to our roads. These include the technical difficulties in ensuring that the vehicle works reliably in the infinite range of traffic, weather and road situations it might encounter; the regulatory challenges in understanding how liability and enforcement might change when drivers are no longer essential for vehicle operation; and the societal changes that may be required for communities to trust and accept automated vehicles as being a valuable part of the mobility landscape.

G   It's clear that there are many challenges that need to be addressed but, through robust and targeted research, these can most probably be conquered within the next 10 years. Mobility will change in such potentially significant ways and in association with so many other technological developments, such as telepresence and virtual reality, that it is hard to make concrete predictions about the future. However, one thing is certain: change is coming, and the need to be flexible in response to this will be vital for those involved in manufacturing the vehicles that will deliver future mobility.

Questions 14–18

Reading Passage 2 has seven sections, **A–G**.

Which section contains the following information?

*Write the correct letter, **A–G**, in boxes 14–18 on your answer sheet.*

14   reference to the amount of time when a car is not in use

15   mention of several advantages of driverless vehicles for individual road-users

16   reference to the opportunity of choosing the most appropriate vehicle for each trip

17   an estimate of how long it will take to overcome a number of problems

18   a suggestion that the use of driverless cars may have no effect on the number of vehicles manufactured

Questions 19–22

Complete the summary below.

*Choose **NO MORE THAN TWO WORDS** from the passage for each answer.*

Write your answers in boxes 19–22 on your answer sheet.

The impact of driverless cars

Figures from the Transport Research Laboratory indicate that most motor accidents are partly due to **19** .... , so the introduction of driverless vehicles will result in greater safety. In addition to the direct benefits of automation, it may bring other advantages. For example, schemes for **20** .... will be more workable, especially in towns and cities, resulting in fewer cars on the road.

According to the University of Michigan Transportation Research Institute, there could be a 43 percent drop in **21** .... of cars. However, this would mean that the yearly **22** .... of each car would, on average, be twice as high as it currently is. This would lead to a higher turnover of vehicles, and therefore no reduction in automotive manufacturing.

Questions 23 and 24

Choose **TWO** letters, **A–E**.

Write the correct letters in boxes 23 and 24 on your answer sheet.

Which **TWO** benefits of automated vehicles does the writer mention?

    A   Car travellers could enjoy considerable cost savings.
    B   It would be easier to find parking spaces in urban areas.
    C   Travellers could spend journeys doing something other than driving.
    D   People who find driving physically difficult could travel independently.
    E   A reduction in the number of cars would mean a reduction in pollution.

Questions 25 and 26

Choose **TWO** letters, **A–E**.

Write the correct letters in boxes 25 and 26 on your answer sheet.

Which **TWO** challenges to automated vehicle development does the writer mention?

    A   making sure the general public has confidence in automated vehicles
    B   managing the pace of transition from conventional to automated vehicles
    C   deciding how to compensate professional drivers who become redundant
    D   setting up the infrastructure to make roads suitable for automated vehicles
    E   getting automated vehicles to adapt to various different driving conditions

→ ◑ p. 120

READING PASSAGE 3

*You should spend about 20 minutes on **Questions 27–40**, which are based on Reading Passage 3 below.*

What is exploration?

We are all explorers. Our desire to discover, and then share that new-found knowledge, is part of what makes us human – indeed, this has played an important part in our success as a species. Long before the first caveman slumped down beside the fire and grunted news that there were plenty of wildebeest over yonder, our ancestors had learnt the value of sending out scouts to investigate the unknown. This questing nature of ours undoubtedly helped our species spread around the globe, just as it nowadays no doubt helps the last nomadic Penan maintain their existence in the depleted forests of Borneo, and a visitor negotiate the subways of New York.

Over the years, we've come to think of explorers as a peculiar breed – different from the rest of us, different from those of us who are merely 'well travelled', even; and perhaps there *is* a type of person more suited to seeking out the new, a type of caveman more inclined to risk venturing out. That, however, doesn't take away from the fact that we all have this enquiring instinct, even today; and that in all sorts of professions – whether artist, marine biologist or astronomer – borders of the unknown are being tested each day.

Thomas Hardy set some of his novels in Egdon Heath, a fictional area of uncultivated land, and used the landscape to suggest the desires and fears of his characters. He is delving into matters we all recognise because they are common to humanity. This is surely an act of exploration, and into a world as remote as the author chooses. Explorer and travel writer Peter Fleming talks of the moment when the explorer returns to the existence he has left behind with his loved ones. The traveller 'who has for weeks or months seen himself only as a puny and irrelevant alien crawling laboriously over a country in which he has no roots and no background, suddenly encounters his other self, a relatively solid figure, with a place in the minds of certain people'.

In this book about the exploration of the earth's surface, I have confined myself to those whose travels were real and who also aimed at more than personal discovery. But that still left me with another problem: the word 'explorer' has become associated with a past era. We think back to a golden age, as if exploration peaked somehow in the 19th century – as if the process of discovery is now on the decline, though the truth is that we have named only one and a half million of this planet's species, and there may be more than 10 million – and that's not including bacteria. We have studied only 5 per cent of the species we know. We have scarcely mapped the ocean floors, and know even less about ourselves; we fully understand the workings of only 10 per cent of our brains.

Here is how some of today's 'explorers' define the word. Ran Fiennes, dubbed the 'greatest living explorer', said, 'An explorer is someone who has done something that no human has done before – and also done something scientifically useful.' Chris Bonington, a leading mountaineer, felt exploration was to be found in the act of physically touching the unknown: 'You have to have gone somewhere new.' Then Robin Hanbury-Tenison, a campaigner on behalf of remote so-called 'tribal' peoples, said, 'A traveller simply records information about some far-off world, and reports back; but an explorer *changes* the world.' Wilfred Thesiger, who crossed Arabia's Empty Quarter in 1946, and belongs to an era of unmechanised travel now lost to the rest of us, told me, 'If I'd gone across by camel when I could have gone by car, it would have been a stunt.' To him, exploration meant bringing back information from a remote place regardless of any great self-discovery.

Each definition is slightly different – and tends to reflect the field of endeavour of each pioneer. It was the same whoever I asked: the prominent historian would say exploration was a thing of the past, the cutting-edge scientist would say it was of the present. And so on. They each set their own particular criteria; the common factor in their approach being that they all had, unlike many of us who simply enjoy travel or discovering new things, both a very definite objective from the outset and also a desire to record their findings.

I'd best declare my own bias. As a writer, I'm interested in the exploration of ideas. I've done a great many expeditions and each one was unique. I've lived for months alone with isolated groups of people all around the world, even two 'uncontacted tribes'. But none of these things is of the slightest interest to anyone unless, through my books, I've found a new slant, explored a new idea. Why? Because the world has moved on. The time has long passed for the great continental voyages – another walk to the poles, another crossing of the Empty Quarter. We know how the land surface of our planet lies; exploration of it is now down to the details – the habits of microbes, say, or the grazing behaviour of buffalo. Aside from the deep sea and deep underground, it's the era of specialists. However, this is to disregard the role the human mind has in conveying remote places; and this is what interests me: how a fresh interpretation, even of a well-travelled route, can give its readers new insights.

Questions 27–32

Choose the correct letter, **A**, **B**, **C** or **D**.

Write the correct letter in boxes 27–32 on your answer sheet.

27   The writer refers to visitors to New York to illustrate the point that

   A   exploration is an intrinsic element of being human.
   B   most people are enthusiastic about exploring.
   C   exploration can lead to surprising results.
   D   most people find exploration daunting.

28   According to the second paragraph, what is the writer's view of explorers?

   A   Their discoveries have brought both benefits and disadvantages.
   B   Their main value is in teaching others.
   C   They act on an urge that is common to everyone.
   D   They tend to be more attracted to certain professions than to others.

29   The writer refers to a description of Egdon Heath to suggest that

   A   Hardy was writing about his own experience of exploration.
   B   Hardy was mistaken about the nature of exploration.
   C   Hardy's aim was to investigate people's emotional states.
   D   Hardy's aim was to show the attraction of isolation.

30   In the fourth paragraph, the writer refers to 'a golden age' to suggest that

   A   the amount of useful information produced by exploration has decreased.
   B   fewer people are interested in exploring than in the 19th century.
   C   recent developments have made exploration less exciting.
   D   we are wrong to think that exploration is no longer necessary.

31   In the sixth paragraph, when discussing the definition of exploration, the writer argues that

   A   people tend to relate exploration to their own professional interests.
   B   certain people are likely to misunderstand the nature of exploration.
   C   the generally accepted definition has changed over time.
   D   historians and scientists have more valid definitions than the general public.

32   In the last paragraph, the writer explains that he is interested in

   A   how someone's personality is reflected in their choice of places to visit.
   B   the human ability to cast new light on places that may be familiar.
   C   how travel writing has evolved to meet changing demands.
   D   the feelings that writers develop about the places that they explore.

Questions 33–37

Look at the following statements (Questions 33–37) and the list of explorers below.

*Match each statement with the correct explorer, **A–E**.*

*Write the correct letter, **A–E**, in boxes 33–37 on your answer sheet.*

NB *You may use any letter more than once.*

33 He referred to the relevance of the form of transport used.

34 He described feelings on coming back home after a long journey.

35 He worked for the benefit of specific groups of people.

36 He did not consider learning about oneself an essential part of exploration.

37 He defined exploration as being both unique and of value to others.

List of Explorers

A   Peter Fleming

B   Ran Fiennes

C   Chris Bonington

D   Robin Hanbury-Tenison

E   Wilfred Thesiger

Questions 38–40

Complete the summary below.

*Choose **NO MORE THAN TWO WORDS** from the passage for each answer.*

Write your answers in boxes 38–40 on your answer sheet.

The writer's own bias

The writer has experience of a large number of **38** .... , and
was the first stranger that certain previously **39** .... people
had encountered. He believes there is no need for further exploration of Earth's
40 .... , except to answer specific questions such as how buffalo eat.

 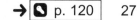

WRITING

WRITING TASK 1

You should spend about 20 minutes on this task.

> **The chart below shows the results of a survey about people's coffee and tea buying and drinking habits in five Australian cities.**
>
> **Summarise the information by selecting and reporting the main features, and make comparisons where relevant.**

Write at least 150 words.

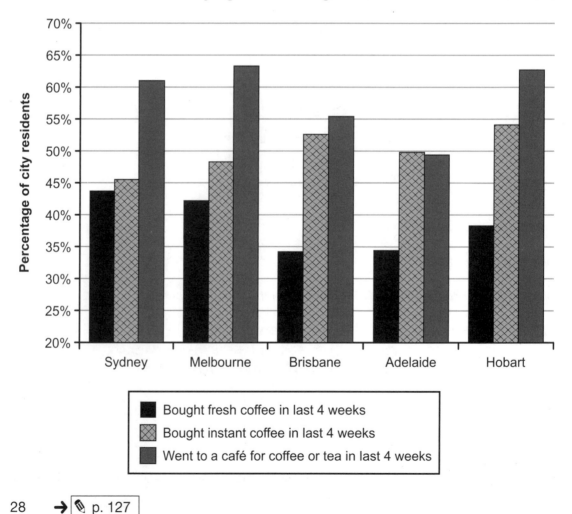

Coffee and tea buying and drinking habits in five cities in Australia

WRITING TASK 2

You should spend about 40 minutes on this task.

Write about the following topic:

> **In some countries, owning a home rather than renting one is very important for people.**
>
> **Why might this be the case?**
>
> **Do you think this is a positive or negative situation?**

Give reasons for your answer and include any relevant examples from your own knowledge or experience.

Write at least 250 words.

SPEAKING

PART 1

The examiner asks the candidate about him/herself, his/her home, work or studies and other familiar topics.

Example Speaking test video

EXAMPLE

Email

- What kinds of emails do you receive about your work or studies?
- Do you prefer to email, phone or text your friends? [Why?]
- Do you reply to emails and messages as soon as you receive them? [Why/Why not?]
- Are you happy to receive emails that are advertising things? [Why/Why not?]

PART 2

Describe a hotel that you know.

You should say:
>   **where this hotel is**
>   **what this hotel looks like**
>   **what facilities this hotel has**

and explain whether you think this is a nice hotel to stay in.

You will have to talk about the topic for one to two minutes. You have one minute to think about what you are going to say. You can make some notes to help you if you wish.

PART 3

Discussion topics:

Staying in hotels

Example questions:
What things are important when people are choosing a hotel?
Why do some people not like staying in hotels?
Do you think staying in a luxury hotel is a waste of money?

Working in a hotel

Example questions:
Do you think hotel work is a good career for life?
How does working in a big hotel compare with working in a small hotel?
What skills are needed to be a successful hotel manager?

Test 2

PART 1   *Questions 1–10*

Questions 1–4

Complete the table below.

*Write **ONE WORD ONLY** for each answer.*

Listening test audio

Festival information		
Date	**Type of event**	**Details**
17th	a concert	performers from Canada
18th	a ballet	company called **1** ....
19th–20th (afternoon)	a play	type of play: a comedy called *Jemima* has had a good **2** ....
20th (evening)	a **3** .... show	show is called **4** ....

Questions 5–10

Complete the notes below.

*Write **ONE WORD ONLY** for each answer.*

Workshops

- Making **5** .... food

- (children only) Making **6** ....

- (adults only) Making toys from **7** .... using various tools

Outdoor activities

- Swimming in the **8** ....

- Walking in the woods, led by an expert on **9** ....

See the festival organiser's **10** .... for more information

---

PART 2   *Questions 11–20*

Questions 11–14

Choose the correct letter, A, B or C.

Listening test audio

Minster Park

11 The park was originally established

    A as an amenity provided by the city council.
    B as land belonging to a private house.
    C as a shared area set up by the local community.

12 Why is there a statue of Diane Gosforth in the park?

    A She was a resident who helped to lead a campaign.
    B She was a council member responsible for giving the public access.
    C She was a senior worker at the park for many years.

13 During the First World War, the park was mainly used for

    A exercises by troops.
    B growing vegetables.
    C public meetings.

14 When did the physical transformation of the park begin?

    A 2013
    B 2015
    C 2016

Questions 15–20

Label the map below.

*Write the correct letter, **A–I**, next to Questions 15–20.*

Minster Park

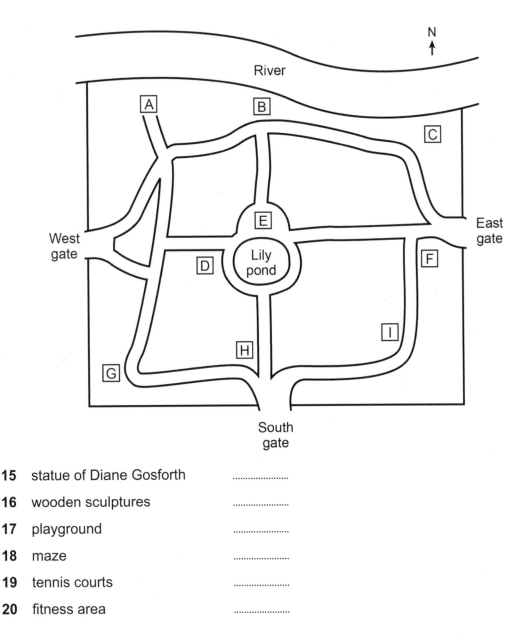

15	statue of Diane Gosforth	....
16	wooden sculptures	....
17	playground	....
18	maze	....
19	tennis courts	....
20	fitness area	....

→ 🔊 p. 121 📄 p. 102

PART 3   *Questions 21–30*

Questions 21 and 22

*Choose **TWO** letters, **A–E**.*

Listening test audio

Which **TWO** groups of people is the display primarily intended for?

    A   students from the English department
    B   residents of the local area
    C   the university's teaching staff
    D   potential new students
    E   students from other departments

Questions 23 and 24

*Choose **TWO** letters, **A–E**.*

What are Cathy and Graham's **TWO** reasons for choosing the novelist Charles Dickens?

    A   His speeches inspired others to try to improve society.
    B   He used his publications to draw attention to social problems.
    C   His novels are well-known now.
    D   He was consulted on a number of social issues.
    E   His reputation has changed in recent times.

Questions 25–30

What topic do Cathy and Graham choose to illustrate with each novel?

*Choose **SIX** answers from the box and write the correct letter, **A–H**, next to Questions 25–30.*

	Topics
A	poverty
B	education
C	Dickens's travels
D	entertainment
E	crime and the law
F	wealth
G	medicine
H	a woman's life

Novels by Dickens

25	*The Pickwick Papers*	....
26	*Oliver Twist*	....
27	*Nicholas Nickleby*	....
28	*Martin Chuzzlewit*	....
29	*Bleak House*	....
30	*Little Dorrit*	....

→ p. 121　 p. 103

PART 4   *Questions 31–40*

Complete the notes below.

Write ONE WORD ONLY for each answer.

Listening test audio

Agricultural programme in Mozambique

How the programme was organised

- It focused on a dry and arid region in Chicualacuala district, near the Limpopo River.

- People depended on the forest to provide charcoal as a source of income.

- **31** .... was seen as the main priority to ensure the supply of water.

- Most of the work organised by farmers' associations was done by **32** ....

- Fenced areas were created to keep animals away from crops.

- The programme provided

  – **33** .... for the fences

  – **34** .... for suitable crops

  – water pumps.

- The farmers provided

  – labour

  – **35** .... for the fences on their land.

Further developments

- The marketing of produce was sometimes difficult due to lack of **36** ....

- Training was therefore provided in methods of food **37** ....

- Farmers made special places where **38** .... could be kept.

- Local people later suggested keeping **39** ....

Evaluation and lessons learned

- Agricultural production increased, improving incomes and food security.

- Enough time must be allowed, particularly for the **40** .... phase of the programme.

READING PASSAGE 1

*You should spend about 20 minutes on **Questions 1–13**, which are based on Reading Passage 1 below.*

Could urban engineers learn from dance?

A   The way we travel around cities has a major impact on whether they are sustainable. Transportation is estimated to account for 30% of energy consumption in most of the world's most developed nations, so lowering the need for energy-using vehicles is essential for decreasing the environmental impact of mobility. But as more and more people move to cities, it is important to think about other kinds of sustainable travel too. The ways we travel affect our physical and mental health, our social lives, our access to work and culture, and the air we breathe. Engineers are tasked with changing how we travel round cities through urban design, but the engineering industry still works on the assumptions that led to the creation of the energy-consuming transport systems we have now: the emphasis placed solely on efficiency, speed, and quantitative data. We need radical changes, to make it healthier, more enjoyable, and less environmentally damaging to travel around cities.

B   Dance might hold some of the answers. That is not to suggest everyone should dance their way to work, however healthy and happy it might make us, but rather that the techniques used by choreographers to experiment with and design movement in dance could provide engineers with tools to stimulate new ideas in city-making. Richard Sennett, an influential urbanist and sociologist who has transformed ideas about the way cities are made, argues that urban design has suffered from a separation between mind and body since the introduction of the architectural blueprint.

C   Whereas medieval builders improvised and adapted construction through their intimate knowledge of materials and personal experience of the conditions on a site, building designs are now conceived and stored in media technologies that detach the designer from the physical and social realities they are creating. While the design practices created by these new technologies are essential for managing the technical complexity of the modern city, they have the drawback of simplifying reality in the process.

D   To illustrate, Sennett discusses the Peachtree Center in Atlanta, USA, a development typical of the modernist approach to urban planning prevalent in the 1970s. Peachtree created a grid of streets and towers intended as a new pedestrian-friendly downtown for Atlanta. According to Sennett, this failed because its designers had invested too much faith in computer-aided design to tell them how it would operate. They failed to take into account that purpose-built street cafés could not operate in the hot sun without the protective awnings common in older buildings, and would need energy-consuming air conditioning instead, or that its giant car park would feel so unwelcoming that it would put people off getting out of their cars. What seems entirely predictable and controllable on screen has unexpected results when translated into reality.

E   The same is true in transport engineering, which uses models to predict and shape the way people move through the city. Again, these models are necessary, but they are built on specific world views in which certain forms of efficiency and safety are considered and other experiences of the city ignored. Designs that seem logical in models appear counter-intuitive in the actual experience of their users. The guard rails that will be familiar to anyone who has attempted to cross a British road, for example, were an engineering solution to pedestrian safety based on models that prioritise the smooth flow of traffic. On wide major roads, they often guide pedestrians to specific crossing points and slow down their progress across the road by using staggered access points to divide the crossing into two – one for each carriageway. In doing so they make crossings feel longer, introducing psychological barriers greatly impacting those that are the least mobile, and encouraging others to make dangerous crossings to get around the guard rails. These barriers don't just make it harder to cross the road: they divide communities and decrease opportunities for healthy transport. As a result, many are now being removed, causing disruption, cost, and waste.

F   If their designers had had the tools to think with their bodies – like dancers – and imagine how these barriers would feel, there might have been a better solution. In order to bring about fundamental changes to the ways we use our cities, engineering will need to develop a richer understanding of why people move in certain ways, and how this movement affects them. Choreography may not seem an obvious choice for tackling this problem. Yet it shares with engineering the aim of designing patterns of movement within limitations of space. It is an art form developed almost entirely by trying out ideas with the body, and gaining instant feedback on how the results feel. Choreographers have deep understanding of the psychological, aesthetic, and physical implications of different ways of moving.

G   Observing the choreographer Wayne McGregor, cognitive scientist David Kirsh described how he 'thinks with the body'. Kirsh argues that by using the body to simulate outcomes, McGregor is able to imagine solutions that would not be possible using purely abstract thought. This kind of physical knowledge is valued in many areas of expertise, but currently has no place in formal engineering design processes. A suggested method for transport engineers is to improvise design solutions and get instant feedback about how they would work from their own experience of them, or model designs at full scale in the way choreographers experiment with groups of dancers. Above all, perhaps, they might learn to design for emotional as well as functional effects.

Questions 1–6

Reading Passage 1 has seven paragraphs, **A–G**.

Which paragraph contains the following information?

*Write the correct letter, **A–G**, in boxes 1–6 on your answer sheet.*

1   reference to an appealing way of using dance that the writer is not proposing

2   an example of a contrast between past and present approaches to building

3   mention of an objective of both dance and engineering

4   reference to an unforeseen problem arising from ignoring the climate

5   why some measures intended to help people are being reversed

6   reference to how transport has an impact on human lives

Questions 7–13

Complete the summary below.

*Choose **ONE WORD ONLY** from the passage for each answer.*

Write your answers in boxes 7–13 on your answer sheet.

Guard rails

Guard rails were introduced on British roads to improve the **7** ....
of pedestrians, while ensuring that the movement of **8** .... is
not disrupted. Pedestrians are led to access points, and encouraged to cross one
9 .... at a time.

An unintended effect is to create psychological difficulties in crossing the road,
particularly for less **10** .... people. Another result is that some
people cross the road in a **11** .... way. The guard rails separate
12 .... , and make it more difficult to introduce forms of transport
that are **13** ....

→ 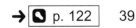 p. 122

READING PASSAGE 2

*You should spend about 20 minutes on **Questions 14–26**, which are based on Reading Passage 2 below.*

Should we try to bring extinct species back to life?

A   The passenger pigeon was a legendary species. Flying in vast numbers across North America, with potentially many millions within a single flock, their migration was once one of nature's great spectacles. Sadly, the passenger pigeon's existence came to an end on 1 September 1914, when the last living specimen died at Cincinnati Zoo. Geneticist Ben Novak is lead researcher on an ambitious project which now aims to bring the bird back to life through a process known as 'de-extinction'. The basic premise involves using cloning technology to turn the DNA of extinct animals into a fertilised embryo, which is carried by the nearest relative still in existence – in this case, the abundant band-tailed pigeon – before being born as a living, breathing animal. Passenger pigeons are one of the pioneering species in this field, but they are far from the only ones on which this cutting-edge technology is being trialled.

B   In Australia, the thylacine, more commonly known as the Tasmanian tiger, is another extinct creature which genetic scientists are striving to bring back to life. 'There is no carnivore now in Tasmania that fills the niche which thylacines once occupied,' explains Michael Archer of the University of New South Wales. He points out that in the decades since the thylacine went extinct, there has been a spread in a 'dangerously debilitating' facial tumour syndrome which threatens the existence of the Tasmanian devils, the island's other notorious resident. Thylacines would have prevented this spread because they would have killed significant numbers of Tasmanian devils. 'If that contagious cancer had popped up previously, it would have burned out in whatever region it started. The return of thylacines to Tasmania could help to ensure that devils are never again subjected to risks of this kind.'

C   If extinct species can be brought back to life, can humanity begin to correct the damage it has caused to the natural world over the past few millennia? 'The idea of de-extinction is that we can reverse this process, bringing species that no longer exist back to life,' says Beth Shapiro of University of California Santa Cruz's Genomics Institute. 'I don't think that we can do this. There is no way to bring back something that is 100 per cent identical to a species that went extinct a long time ago.' A more practical approach for long-extinct species is to take the DNA of existing species as a template, ready for the insertion of strands of extinct animal DNA to create something new; a hybrid, based on the living species, but which looks and/or acts like the animal which died out.

D   This complicated process and questionable outcome begs the question: what is the actual point of this technology? 'For us, the goal has always been replacing the extinct species with a suitable replacement,' explains Novak. 'When it comes to breeding, band-tailed pigeons scatter and make maybe one or two nests per hectare, whereas passenger pigeons were very social and would make 10,000 or more nests in one hectare.' Since the disappearance of this key species, ecosystems in the eastern US have suffered, as the lack of disturbance caused by thousands of passenger pigeons wrecking trees and branches means there has been minimal need for regrowth. This has left forests stagnant and therefore unwelcoming to the plants and animals which evolved to help regenerate the forest after a disturbance. According to Novak, a hybridised band-tailed pigeon, with the added nesting habits of a passenger pigeon, could, in theory, re-establish that forest disturbance, thereby creating a habitat necessary for a great many other native species to thrive.

E   Another popular candidate for this technology is the woolly mammoth. George Church, professor at Harvard Medical School and leader of the Woolly Mammoth Revival Project, has been focusing on cold resistance, the main way in which the extinct woolly mammoth and its nearest living relative, the Asian elephant, differ. By pinpointing which genetic traits made it possible for mammoths to survive the icy climate of the tundra, the project's goal is to return mammoths, or a mammoth-like species, to the area. 'My highest priority would be preserving the endangered Asian elephant,' says Church, 'expanding their range to the huge ecosystem of the tundra. Necessary adaptations would include smaller ears, thicker hair, and extra insulating fat, all for the purpose of reducing heat loss in the tundra, and all traits found in the now extinct woolly mammoth.' This repopulation of the tundra and boreal forests of Eurasia and North America with large mammals could also be a useful factor in reducing carbon emissions – elephants punch holes through snow and knock down trees, which encourages grass growth. This grass growth would reduce temperatures, and mitigate emissions from melting permafrost.

F   While the prospect of bringing extinct animals back to life might capture imaginations, it is, of course, far easier to try to save an existing species which is merely threatened with extinction. 'Many of the technologies that people have in mind when they think about de-extinction can be used as a form of "genetic rescue",' explains Shapiro. She prefers to focus the debate on how this emerging technology could be used to fully understand why various species went extinct in the first place, and therefore how we could use it to make genetic modifications which could prevent mass extinctions in the future. 'I would also say there's an incredible moral hazard to not do anything at all,' she continues. 'We know that what we are doing today is not enough, and we have to be willing to take some calculated and measured risks.'

Questions 14–17

Reading Passage 2 has six paragraphs, **A–F**.

Which paragraph contains the following information?

*Write the correct letter, **A–F**, in boxes 14–17 on your answer sheet.*

NB *You may use any letter more than once.*

14 a reference to how further disappearance of multiple species could be avoided

15 explanation of a way of reproducing an extinct animal using the DNA of only that species

16 reference to a habitat which has suffered following the extinction of a species

17 mention of the exact point at which a particular species became extinct

Questions 18–22

Complete the summary below.

*Choose **NO MORE THAN TWO WORDS** from the passage for each answer.*

Write your answers in boxes 18–22 on your answer sheet.

The woolly mammoth revival project

Professor George Church and his team are trying to identify the
18 .... which enabled mammoths to live in the tundra. The findings could help preserve the mammoth's close relative, the endangered Asian elephant.

According to Church, introducing Asian elephants to the tundra would involve certain physical adaptations to minimise **19** .... To survive in the tundra, the species would need to have the mammoth-like features of thicker hair, **20** .... of a reduced size and more **21** ....

Repopulating the tundra with mammoths or Asian elephant/mammoth hybrids would also have an impact on the environment, which could help to reduce temperatures and decrease **22** ....

Questions 23–26

Look at the following statements (Questions 23–26) and the list of people below.

*Match each statement with the correct person, **A**, **B** or **C**.*

*Write the correct letter, **A**, **B** or **C**, in boxes 23–26 on your answer sheet.*

NB *You may use any letter more than once.*

23 Reintroducing an extinct species to its original habitat could improve the health of a particular species living there.

24 It is important to concentrate on the causes of an animal's extinction.

25 A species brought back from extinction could have an important beneficial impact on the vegetation of its habitat.

26 Our current efforts at preserving biodiversity are insufficient.

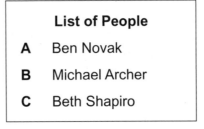

	List of People
A	Ben Novak
B	Michael Archer
C	Beth Shapiro

→ 🔊 p. 122

READING PASSAGE 3

*You should spend about 20 minutes on **Questions 27–40**, which are based on Reading Passage 3 below.*

Having a laugh

The findings of psychological scientists reveal the importance of humour

Humans start developing a sense of humour as early as six weeks old, when babies begin to laugh and smile in response to stimuli. Laughter is universal across all human cultures and even exists in some form in rats, chimps, and bonobos. Like other human emotions and expressions, laughter and humour provide psychological scientists with rich resources for studying human psychology, ranging from the development of language to the neuroscience of social perception.

Theories focusing on the evolution of laughter point to it as an important adaptation for social communication. Take, for example, the recorded laughter in TV comedy shows. Back in 1950, US sound engineer Charley Douglass hated dealing with the unpredictable laughter of live audiences, so started recording his own 'laugh tracks'. These were intended to help people at home feel like they were in a social situation, such as a crowded theatre. Douglass even recorded various types of laughter, as well as mixtures of laughter from men, women, and children. In doing so, he picked up on a quality of laughter that is now interesting researchers: a simple 'haha' communicates a remarkable amount of socially relevant information.

In one study conducted in 2016, samples of laughter from pairs of English-speaking students were recorded at the University of California, Santa Cruz. A team made up of more than 30 psychological scientists, anthropologists, and biologists then played these recordings to listeners from 24 diverse societies, from indigenous tribes in New Guinea to city-dwellers in India and Europe. Participants were asked whether they thought the people laughing were friends or strangers. On average, the results were remarkably consistent: worldwide, people's guesses were correct approximately 60% of the time.

Researchers have also found that different types of laughter serve as codes to complex human social hierarchies. A team led by Christopher Oveis from the University of California, San Diego, found that high-status individuals had different laughs from low-status individuals, and that strangers' judgements of an individual's social status were influenced by the dominant or submissive quality of their laughter. In their study, 48 male college students were randomly assigned to groups of four, with each group composed of two low-status members, who had just joined their college fraternity group, and two high-status members, older students who had been active in the fraternity for at least two years. Laughter was recorded as each student took a turn at being teased by the others, involving the use of mildly insulting nicknames. Analysis revealed that, as expected, high-status individuals produced more dominant laughs and fewer submissive laughs relative to the low-status individuals. Meanwhile, low-status individuals were more likely to change their laughter based on their position of power; that is, the newcomers produced more dominant laughs when they were in the 'powerful' role of teasers. Dominant laughter was higher in pitch, louder, and more variable in tone than submissive laughter.

A random group of volunteers then listened to an equal number of dominant and submissive laughs from both the high- and low-status individuals, and were asked to estimate the social status of the laugher. In line with predictions, laughers producing dominant laughs were perceived to be significantly higher in status than laughers producing submissive laughs. 'This was particularly true for low-status individuals, who were rated as significantly higher in status when displaying a dominant versus submissive laugh,' Oveis and colleagues note. 'Thus, by strategically displaying more dominant laughter when the context allows, low-status individuals may achieve higher status in the eyes of others.' However, high-status individuals were rated as high-status whether they produced their natural dominant laugh or tried to do a submissive one.

Another study, conducted by David Cheng and Lu Wang of Australian National University, was based on the hypothesis that humour might provide a respite from tedious situations in the workplace. This 'mental break' might facilitate the replenishment of mental resources. To test this theory, the researchers recruited 74 business students, ostensibly for an experiment on perception. First, the students performed a tedious task in which they had to cross out every instance of the letter 'e' over two pages of text. The students then were randomly assigned to watch a video clip eliciting either humour, contentment, or neutral feelings. Some watched a clip of the BBC comedy *Mr. Bean*, others a relaxing scene with dolphins swimming in the ocean, and others a factual video about the management profession.

The students then completed a task requiring persistence in which they were asked to guess the potential performance of employees based on provided profiles, and were told that making 10 correct assessments in a row would lead to a win. However, the software was programmed such that it was nearly impossible to achieve 10 consecutive correct answers. Participants were allowed to quit the task at any point. Students who had watched the *Mr. Bean* video ended up spending significantly more time working on the task, making twice as many predictions as the other two groups.

Cheng and Wang then replicated these results in a second study, during which they had participants complete long multiplication questions by hand. Again, participants who watched the humorous video spent significantly more time working on this tedious task and completed more questions correctly than did the students in either of the other groups.

'Although humour has been found to help relieve stress and facilitate social relationships, the traditional view of task performance implies that individuals should avoid things such as humour that may distract them from the accomplishment of task goals,' Cheng and Wang conclude. 'We suggest that humour is not only enjoyable but more importantly, energising.'

Questions 27–31

*Choose the correct letter, **A**, **B**, **C** or **D**.*

Write the correct letter in boxes 27–31 on your answer sheet.

27   When referring to laughter in the first paragraph, the writer emphasises

    A   its impact on language.
    B   its function in human culture.
    C   its value to scientific research.
    D   its universality in animal societies.

28   What does the writer suggest about Charley Douglass?

    A   He understood the importance of enjoying humour in a group setting.
    B   He believed that TV viewers at home needed to be told when to laugh.
    C   He wanted his shows to appeal to audiences across the social spectrum.
    D   He preferred shows where audiences were present in the recording studio.

29   What makes the Santa Cruz study particularly significant?

    A   the various different types of laughter that were studied
    B   the similar results produced by a wide range of cultures
    C   the number of different academic disciplines involved
    D   the many kinds of people whose laughter was recorded

30   Which of the following happened in the San Diego study?

    A   Some participants became very upset.
    B   Participants exchanged roles.
    C   Participants who had not met before became friends.
    D   Some participants were unable to laugh.

31   In the fifth paragraph, what did the results of the San Diego study suggest?

    A   It is clear whether a dominant laugh is produced by a high- or low-status person.
    B   Low-status individuals in a position of power will still produce submissive laughs.
    C   The submissive laughs of low- and high-status individuals are surprisingly similar.
    D   High-status individuals can always be identified by their way of laughing.

Questions 32–36

*Complete the summary using the list of words, **A–H**, below.*

*Write the correct letter, **A–H**, in boxes 32–36 on your answer sheet.*

The benefits of humour

In one study at Australian National University, randomly chosen groups of participants were shown one of three videos, each designed to generate a different kind of **32** .... When all participants were then given a deliberately frustrating task to do, it was found that those who had watched the **33** .... video persisted with the task for longer and tried harder to accomplish the task than either of the other two groups.

A second study in which participants were asked to perform a particularly **34** .... task produced similar results. According to researchers David Cheng and Lu Wang, these findings suggest that humour not only reduces **35** .... and helps build social connections but it may also have a **36** .... effect on the body and mind.

A	laughter	**B**	relaxing	**C**	boring
D	anxiety	**E**	stimulating	**F**	emotion
G	enjoyment	**H**	amusing		

Questions 37–40

Do the following statements agree with the claims of the writer in Reading Passage 3?

In boxes 37–40 on your answer sheet, write

> **YES**   *if the statement agrees with the claims of the writer*
> **NO**   *if the statement contradicts the claims of the writer*
> **NOT GIVEN**   *if it is impossible to say what the writer thinks about this*

37 Participants in the Santa Cruz study were more accurate at identifying the laughs of friends than those of strangers.

38 The researchers in the San Diego study were correct in their predictions regarding the behaviour of the high-status individuals.

39 The participants in the Australian National University study were given a fixed amount of time to complete the task focusing on employee profiles.

40 Cheng and Wang's conclusions were in line with established notions regarding task performance.

WRITING TASK 1

You should spend about 20 minutes on this task.

> *The graph below shows the number of tourists visiting a particular Caribbean island between 2010 and 2017.*
>
> *Summarise the information by selecting and reporting the main features, and make comparisons where relevant.*

Write at least 150 words.

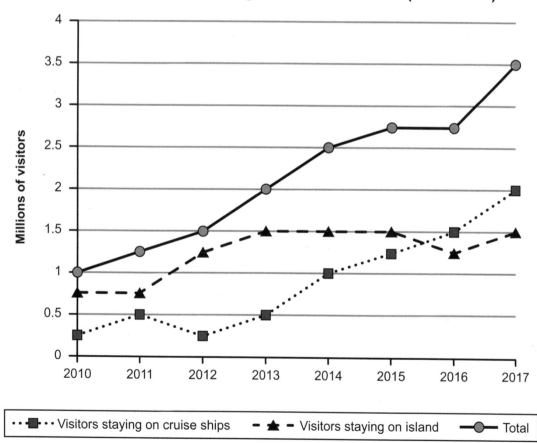

Number of tourists visiting a Caribbean island (2010–2017)

WRITING TASK 2

You should spend about 40 minutes on this task.

Write about the following topic:

> *In the future, nobody will buy printed newspapers or books because they will be able to read everything they want online without paying.*
>
> *To what extent do you agree or disagree with this statement?*

Give reasons for your answer and include any relevant examples from your own knowledge or experience.

Write at least 250 words.

SPEAKING

PART 1

The examiner asks the candidate about him/herself, his/her home, work or studies and other familiar topics.

EXAMPLE

Languages

- How many languages can you speak? [Why/Why not?]
- How useful will English be to you in your future? [Why/Why not?]
- What do you remember about learning languages at school? [Why/Why not?]
- What do you think would be the hardest language for you to learn? [Why?]

PART 2

Describe a website that you bought something from.

You should say:
   what the website is
   what you bought from this website
   how satisfied you were with what you bought

and explain what you liked or disliked about using this website.

You will have to talk about the topic for one to two minutes. You have one minute to think about what you are going to say. You can make some notes to help you if you wish.

PART 3

Discussion topics:

Shopping online

Example questions:
What kinds of things do people in your country often buy from online shops?
Why do you think online shopping has become so popular nowadays?
What are some possible disadvantages of buying things from online shops?

The culture of consumerism

Example questions:
Why do many people today keep buying things which they do not need?
Do you believe the benefits of a consumer society outweigh the disadvantages?
How possible is it to avoid the culture of consumerism?

Test 3

PART 1   *Questions 1–10*

Complete the notes below.

*Write **ONE WORD AND/OR A NUMBER** for each answer.*

Listening test audio

Employment Agency: Possible Jobs

First Job

Administrative assistant in a company that produces **1** .... (North London)

Responsibilities

- data entry
- go to **2** .... and take notes
- general admin
- management of **3** ....

Requirements

- good computer skills including spreadsheets
- good interpersonal skills
- attention to **4** ....

Experience

- need a minimum of **5** .... of experience of teleconferencing

---

Second Job

Warehouse assistant in South London

Responsibilities

- stock management
- managing **6** ....

Requirements

- ability to work with numbers
- good computer skills
- very organised and **7** ....
- good communication skills
- used to working in a **8** ....
- able to cope with items that are **9** ....

Need experience of

- driving in London
- warehouse work
- **10** .... service

PART 2   *Questions 11–20*

Questions 11–16

*Choose the correct letter, **A**, **B** or **C**.*

Street Play Scheme

11   When did the Street Play Scheme first take place?

  A   two years ago
  B   three years ago
  C   six years ago

12   How often is Beechwood Road closed to traffic now?

  A   once a week
  B   on Saturdays and Sundays
  C   once a month

13   Who is responsible for closing the road?

  A   a council official
  B   the police
  C   local wardens

14   Residents who want to use their cars

  A   have to park in another street.
  B   must drive very slowly.
  C   need permission from a warden.

15   Alice says that Street Play Schemes are most needed in

  A   wealthy areas.
  B   quiet suburban areas.
  C   areas with heavy traffic.

16   What has been the reaction of residents who are not parents?

  A   Many of them were unhappy at first.
  B   They like seeing children play in the street.
  C   They are surprised by the lack of noise.

Questions 17 and 18

Choose **TWO** letters, **A–E**.

Which **TWO** benefits for children does Alice think are the most important?

    A   increased physical activity
    B   increased sense of independence
    C   opportunity to learn new games
    D   opportunity to be part of a community
    E   opportunity to make new friends

Questions 19 and 20

Choose **TWO** letters, **A–E**.

Which **TWO** results of the King Street experiment surprised Alice?

    A   more shoppers
    B   improved safety
    C   less air pollution
    D   more relaxed atmosphere
    E   less noise pollution

PART 3   *Questions 21–30*

Questions 21–26

Complete the notes below.

*Write **ONE WORD ONLY** for each answer.*

Listening test audio

What Hazel should analyse about items in newspapers:

- what **21** .... the item is on

- the **22** .... of the item, including the headline

- any **23** .... accompanying the item

- the **24** .... of the item, e.g. what's made prominent

- the writer's main **25** ....

- the **26** .... the writer may make about the reader

Questions 27–30

What does Hazel decide to do about each of the following types of articles?

*Write the correct letter, **A**, **B** or **C**, next to Questions 27–30.*

> **A**   She will definitely look for a suitable article.
>
> **B**   She may look for a suitable article.
>
> **C**   She definitely won't look for an article.

Types of articles

27 national news item   ....

28 editorial   ....

29 human interest   ....

30 arts   ....

PART 4   *Questions 31–40*

Complete the notes below.

*Write **ONE WORD ONLY** for each answer.*

Listening test audio

Early history of keeping clean

Prehistoric times:

- water was used to wash off **31** ....

Ancient Babylon:

- soap-like material found in **32** .... cylinders

Ancient Greece:

- people cleaned themselves with sand and other substances

- used a strigil – scraper made of **33** ....

- washed clothes in streams

Ancient Germany and Gaul:

- used soap to colour their **34** ....

Ancient Rome:

- animal fat, ashes and clay mixed through action of rain, used for washing clothes

- from about 312 BC, water carried to Roman **35** .... by aqueducts

Europe in Middle Ages:

- decline in bathing contributed to occurrence of **36** ....

- **37** .... began to be added to soap

Europe from 17th century:

- 1600s: cleanliness and bathing started becoming usual

- 1791: Leblanc invented a way of making soda ash from **38** ....

- early 1800s: Chevreul turned soapmaking into a **39** ....

- from 1800s, there was no longer a **40** .... on soap

READING

READING PASSAGE 1

*You should spend about 20 minutes on **Questions 1–13**, which are based on Reading Passage 1 below.*

Henry Moore (1898–1986)

The British sculptor Henry Moore was a leading figure in the 20th-century art world

Henry Moore was born in Castleford, a small town near Leeds in the north of England. He was the seventh child of Raymond Moore and his wife Mary Baker. He studied at Castleford Grammar School from 1909 to 1915, where his early interest in art was encouraged by his teacher Alice Gostick. After leaving school, Moore hoped to become a sculptor, but instead he complied with his father's wish that he train as a schoolteacher. He had to abandon his training in 1917 when he was sent to France to fight in the First World War.

After the war, Moore enrolled at the Leeds School of Art, where he studied for two years. In his first year, he spent most of his time drawing. Although he wanted to study sculpture, no teacher was appointed until his second year. At the end of that year, he passed the sculpture examination and was awarded a scholarship to the Royal College of Art in London. In September 1921, he moved to London and began three years of advanced study in sculpture.

Alongside the instruction he received at the Royal College, Moore visited many of the London museums, particularly the British Museum, which had a wide-ranging collection of ancient sculpture. During these visits, he discovered the power and beauty of ancient Egyptian and African sculpture. As he became increasingly interested in these 'primitive' forms of art, he turned away from European sculptural traditions.

After graduating, Moore spent the first six months of 1925 travelling in France. When he visited the Trocadero Museum in Paris, he was impressed by a cast of a Mayan[*] sculpture of the rain spirit. It was a male reclining figure with its knees drawn up together, and its head at a right angle to its body. Moore became fascinated with this stone sculpture, which he thought had a power and originality that no other stone sculpture possessed. He himself started carving a variety of subjects in stone, including depictions of reclining women, mother-and-child groups, and masks.

Moore's exceptional talent soon gained recognition, and in 1926 he started work as a sculpture instructor at the Royal College. In 1933, he became a member of a group of young artists called Unit One. The aim of the group was to convince the English public of the merits of the emerging international movement in modern art and architecture.

---

[*]Mayan: belonging to an ancient civilisation that inhabited parts of current-day Mexico, Guatemala, Belize, El Salvador and Honduras.

Around this time, Moore moved away from the human figure to experiment with abstract shapes. In 1931, he held an exhibition at the Leicester Galleries in London. His work was enthusiastically welcomed by fellow sculptors, but the reviews in the press were extremely negative and turned Moore into a notorious figure. There were calls for his resignation from the Royal College, and the following year, when his contract expired, he left to start a sculpture department at the Chelsea School of Art in London.

Throughout the 1930s, Moore did not show any inclination to please the British public. He became interested in the paintings of the Spanish artist Pablo Picasso, whose work inspired him to distort the human body in a radical way. At times, he seemed to abandon the human figure altogether. The pages of his sketchbooks from this period show his ideas for abstract sculptures that bore little resemblance to the human form.

In 1940, during the Second World War, Moore stopped teaching at the Chelsea School and moved to a farmhouse about 20 miles north of London. A shortage of materials forced him to focus on drawing. He did numerous small sketches of Londoners, later turning these ideas into large coloured drawings in his studio. In 1942, he returned to Castleford to make a series of sketches of the miners who worked there.

In 1944, Harlow, a town near London, offered Moore a commission for a sculpture depicting a family. The resulting work signifies a dramatic change in Moore's style, away from the experimentation of the 1930s towards a more natural and humanistic subject matter. He did dozens of studies in clay for the sculpture, and these were cast in bronze and issued in editions of seven to nine copies each. In this way, Moore's work became available to collectors all over the world. The boost to his income enabled him to take on ambitious projects and start working on the scale he felt his sculpture demanded.

Critics who had begun to think that Moore had become less revolutionary were proven wrong by the appearance, in 1950, of the first of Moore's series of standing figures in bronze, with their harsh and angular pierced forms and distinct impression of menace. Moore also varied his subject matter in the 1950s with such works as *Warrior with Shield* and *Falling Warrior*. These were rare examples of Moore's use of the male figure and owe something to his visit to Greece in 1951, when he had the opportunity to study ancient works of art.

In his final years, Moore created the Henry Moore Foundation to promote art appreciation and to display his work. Moore was the first modern English sculptor to achieve international critical acclaim and he is still regarded as one of the most important sculptors of the 20th century.

Questions 1–7

Do the following statements agree with the information given in Reading Passage 1?

In boxes 1–7 on your answer sheet, write

> **TRUE**   *if the statement agrees with the information*
> **FALSE**   *if the statement contradicts the information*
> **NOT GIVEN** *if there is no information on this*

1   On leaving school, Moore did what his father wanted him to do.

2   Moore began studying sculpture in his first term at the Leeds School of Art.

3   When Moore started at the Royal College of Art, its reputation for teaching sculpture was excellent.

4   Moore became aware of ancient sculpture as a result of visiting London museums.

5   The Trocadero Museum's Mayan sculpture attracted a lot of public interest.

6   Moore thought the Mayan sculpture was similar in certain respects to other stone sculptures.

7   The artists who belonged to Unit One wanted to make modern art and architecture more popular.

Questions 8–13

Complete the notes below.

*Choose **ONE WORD ONLY** from the passage for each answer.*

Write your answers in boxes 8–13 on your answer sheet.

Moore's career as an artist

1930s

* Moore's exhibition at the Leicester Galleries is criticised by the press

* Moore is urged to offer his **8** .... and leave the Royal College

1940s

* Moore turns to drawing because **9** .... for sculpting are not readily available

* While visiting his hometown, Moore does some drawings of
  10 ....

* Moore is employed to produce a sculpture of a **11** ....

* **12** .... start to buy Moore's work

* Moore's increased **13** .... makes it possible for him to do more ambitious sculptures

1950s

* Moore's series of bronze figures marks a further change in his style

---

→ ⬛ p. 124

READING PASSAGE 2

*You should spend about 20 minutes on **Questions 14–26**, which are based on Reading Passage 2 on pages 63 and 64.*

Questions 14–20

Reading Passage 2 has seven sections, **A–G**.

Choose the correct heading for each section from the list of headings below.

*Write the correct number, **i–x**, in boxes 14–20 on your answer sheet.*

List of Headings

i Getting the finance for production

ii An unexpected benefit

iii From initial inspiration to new product

iv The range of potential customers for the device

v What makes the device different from alternatives

vi Cleaning water from a range of sources

vii Overcoming production difficulties

viii Profit not the primary goal

ix A warm welcome for the device

x The number of people affected by water shortages

---

14 Section **A**

15 Section **B**

16 Section **C**

17 Section **D**

18 Section **E**

19 Section **F**

20 Section **G**

The Desolenator: producing clean water

A   Travelling around Thailand in the 1990s, William Janssen was impressed with the basic rooftop solar heating systems that were on many homes, where energy from the sun was absorbed by a plate and then used to heat water for domestic use. Two decades later Janssen developed that basic idea he saw in Southeast Asia into a portable device that uses the power from the sun to purify water.

B   The Desolenator operates as a mobile desalination unit that can take water from different places, such as the sea, rivers, boreholes and rain, and purify it for human consumption. It is particularly valuable in regions where natural groundwater reserves have been polluted, or where seawater is the only water source available.

Janssen saw that there was a need for a sustainable way to clean water in both the developing and the developed countries when he moved to the United Arab Emirates and saw large-scale water processing. 'I was confronted with the enormous carbon footprint that the Gulf nations have because of all of the desalination that they do,' he says.

C   The Desolenator can produce 15 litres of drinking water per day, enough to sustain a family for cooking and drinking. Its main selling point is that unlike standard desalination techniques, it doesn't require a generated power supply: just sunlight. It measures 120 cm by 90 cm, and is easy to transport, thanks to its two wheels. Water enters through a pipe, and flows as a thin film between a sheet of double glazing and the surface of a solar panel, where it is heated by the sun. The warm water flows into a small boiler (heated by a solar-powered battery) where it is converted to steam. When the steam cools, it becomes distilled water. The device has a very simple filter to trap particles, and this can easily be shaken to remove them. There are two tubes for liquid coming out: one for the waste – salt from seawater, fluoride, etc. – and another for the distilled water. The performance of the unit is shown on an LCD screen and transmitted to the company which provides servicing when necessary.

D   A recent analysis found that at least two-thirds of the world's population lives with severe water scarcity for at least a month every year. Janssen says that by 2030 half of the world's population will be living with water stress – where the demand exceeds the supply over a certain period of time. 'It is really important that a sustainable solution is brought to the market that is able to help these people,' he says. Many countries 'don't have the money for desalination plants, which are very expensive to build. They don't have the money to operate them, they are very maintenance intensive, and they don't have the money to buy the diesel to run the desalination plants, so it is a really bad situation.'

E The device is aimed at a wide variety of users – from homeowners in the developing world who do not have a constant supply of water to people living off the grid in rural parts of the US. The first commercial versions of the Desolenator are expected to be in operation in India early next year, after field tests are carried out. The market for the self-sufficient devices in developing countries is twofold – those who cannot afford the money for the device outright and pay through microfinance, and middle-income homes that can lease their own equipment. 'People in India don't pay for a fridge outright; they pay for it over six months. They would put the Desolenator on their roof and hook it up to their municipal supply and they would get very reliable drinking water on a daily basis,' Janssen says. In the developed world, it is aimed at niche markets where tap water is unavailable – for camping, on boats, or for the military, for instance.

F Prices will vary according to where it is bought. In the developing world, the price will depend on what deal aid organisations can negotiate. In developed countries, it is likely to come in at $1,000 (£685) a unit, said Janssen. 'We are a venture with a social mission. We are aware that the product we have envisioned is mainly finding application in the developing world and humanitarian sector and that this is the way we will proceed. We do realise, though, that to be a viable company there is a bottom line to keep in mind,' he says.

G The company itself is based at Imperial College London, although Janssen, its chief executive, still lives in the UAE. It has raised £340,000 in funding so far. Within two years, he says, the company aims to be selling 1,000 units a month, mainly in the humanitarian field. They are expected to be sold in areas such as Australia, northern Chile, Peru, Texas and California.

Questions 21–26

Complete the summary below.

*Choose **ONE WORD ONLY** from the passage for each answer.*

Write your answers in boxes 21–26 on your answer sheet.

How the Desolenator works

The energy required to operate the Desolenator comes from sunlight. The device can be used in different locations, as it has **21** .... Water is fed into a pipe, and a **22** .... of water flows over a solar panel. The water then enters a boiler, where it turns into steam. Any particles in the water are caught in a **23** .... The purified water comes out through one tube, and all types of **24** .... come out through another. A screen displays the **25** .... of the device, and transmits the information to the company so that they know when the Desolenator requires **26** ....

READING PASSAGE 3

*You should spend about 20 minutes on **Questions 27–40**, which are based on Reading Passage 3 below.*

Why fairy tales are really scary tales

Some people think that fairy tales are just stories to amuse children, but their universal and enduring appeal may be due to more serious reasons

People of every culture tell each other fairy tales but the same story often takes a variety of forms in different parts of the world. In the story of *Little Red Riding Hood* that European children are familiar with, a young girl on the way to see her grandmother meets a wolf and tells him where she is going. The wolf runs on ahead and disposes of the grandmother, then gets into bed dressed in the grandmother's clothes to wait for Little Red Riding Hood. You may think you know the story – but which version? In some versions, the wolf swallows up the grandmother, while in others it locks her in a cupboard. In some stories Red Riding Hood gets the better of the wolf on her own, while in others a hunter or a woodcutter hears her cries and comes to her rescue.

The universal appeal of these tales is frequently attributed to the idea that they contain cautionary messages: in the case of *Little Red Riding Hood*, to listen to your mother, and avoid talking to strangers. 'It might be what we find interesting about this story is that it's got this survival-relevant information in it,' says anthropologist Jamie Tehrani at Durham University in the UK. But his research suggests otherwise. 'We have this huge gap in our knowledge about the history and prehistory of storytelling, despite the fact that we know this genre is an incredibly ancient one,' he says. That hasn't stopped anthropologists, folklorists[*] and other academics devising theories to explain the importance of fairy tales in human society. Now Tehrani has found a way to test these ideas, borrowing a technique from evolutionary biologists.

To work out the evolutionary history, development and relationships among groups of organisms, biologists compare the characteristics of living species in a process called 'phylogenetic analysis'. Tehrani has used the same approach to compare related versions of fairy tales to discover how they have evolved and which elements have survived longest.

Tehrani's analysis focused on *Little Red Riding Hood* in its many forms, which include another Western fairy tale known as *The Wolf and the Kids*. Checking for variants of these two tales and similar stories from Africa, East Asia and other regions, he ended up with 58 stories recorded from oral traditions. Once his phylogenetic analysis had established that they were indeed related, he used the same methods to explore how they have developed and altered over time.

First he tested some assumptions about which aspects of the story alter least as it evolves, indicating their importance. Folklorists believe that what happens in a story is more central to the story than the characters in it – that visiting a relative, only to be met by a scary animal in disguise, is

---

[*]Folklorists: those who study traditional stories

more fundamental than whether the visitor is a little girl or three siblings, or the animal is a tiger instead of a wolf.

However, Tehrani found no significant difference in the rate of evolution of incidents compared with that of characters. 'Certain episodes are very stable because they are crucial to the story, but there are lots of other details that can evolve quite freely,' he says. Neither did his analysis support the theory that the central section of a story is the most conserved part. He found no significant difference in the flexibility of events there compared with the beginning or the end.

But the really big surprise came when he looked at the cautionary elements of the story. 'Studies on hunter-gatherer folk tales suggest that these narratives include really important information about the environment and the possible dangers that may be faced there – stuff that's relevant to survival,' he says. Yet in his analysis such elements were just as flexible as seemingly trivial details. What, then, is important enough to be reproduced from generation to generation?

The answer, it would appear, is fear – blood-thirsty and gruesome aspects of the story, such as the eating of the grandmother by the wolf, turned out to be the best preserved of all. Why are these details retained by generations of storytellers, when other features are not? Tehrani has an idea: 'In an oral context, a story won't survive because of one great teller. It also needs to be interesting when it's told by someone who's not necessarily a great storyteller.' Maybe being swallowed whole by a wolf, then cut out of its stomach alive is so gripping that it helps the story remain popular, no matter how badly it's told.

Jack Zipes at the University of Minnesota, Minneapolis, is unconvinced by Tehrani's views on fairy tales. 'Even if they're gruesome, they won't stick unless they matter,' he says. He believes the perennial theme of women as victims in stories like *Little Red Riding Hood* explains why they continue to feel relevant. But Tehrani points out that although this is often the case in Western versions, it is not always true elsewhere. In Chinese and Japanese versions, often known as *The Tiger Grandmother*, the villain is a woman, and in both Iran and Nigeria, the victim is a boy.

Mathias Clasen at Aarhus University in Denmark isn't surprised by Tehrani's findings. 'Habits and morals change, but the things that scare us, and the fact that we seek out entertainment that's designed to scare us – those are constant,' he says. Clasen believes that scary stories teach us what it feels like to be afraid without having to experience real danger, and so build up resistance to negative emotions.

Questions 27–31

*Complete each sentence with the correct ending, **A–F**, below.*

*Write the correct letter, **A–F**, in boxes 27–31 on your answer sheet.*

27 In fairy tales, details of the plot

28 Tehrani rejects the idea that the useful lessons for life in fairy tales

29 Various theories about the social significance of fairy tales

30 Insights into the development of fairy tales

31 All the fairy tales analysed by Tehrani

A	may be provided through methods used in biological research.
B	are the reason for their survival.
C	show considerable global variation.
D	contain animals which transform to become humans.
E	were originally spoken rather than written.
F	have been developed without factual basis.

*Complete the summary using the list of words, **A–I**, below.*

*Write the correct letter, **A–I**, in boxes 32–36 on your answer sheet.*

Phylogenetic analysis of *Little Red Riding Hood*

Tehrani used techniques from evolutionary biology to find out if **32** ....
existed among 58 stories from around the world. He also wanted to know which
aspects of the stories had fewest **33** .... , as he believed these aspects
would be the most important ones. Contrary to other beliefs, he found that some
34 .... that were included in a story tended to change over time,
and that the middle of a story seemed no more important than the other parts.
He was also surprised that parts of a story which seemed to provide some sort of
35 .... were unimportant. The aspect that he found most important in a
story's survival was **36** ....

A	ending	**B**	events	**C**	warning
D	links	**E**	records	**F**	variations
G	horror	**H**	people	**I**	plot

Questions 37–40

*Choose the correct letter, **A**, **B**, **C** or **D**.*

Write the correct letter in boxes 37–40 on your answer sheet.

37   What method did Jamie Tehrani use to test his ideas about fairy tales?

    A   He compared oral and written forms of the same stories.
    B   He looked at many different forms of the same basic story.
    C   He looked at unrelated stories from many different countries.
    D   He contrasted the development of fairy tales with that of living creatures.

38   When discussing Tehrani's views, Jack Zipes suggests that

    A   Tehrani ignores key changes in the role of women.
    B   stories which are too horrific are not always taken seriously.
    C   Tehrani overemphasises the importance of violence in stories.
    D   features of stories only survive if they have a deeper significance.

39   Why does Tehrani refer to Chinese and Japanese fairy tales?

    A   to indicate that Jack Zipes' theory is incorrect
    B   to suggest that crime is a global problem
    C   to imply that all fairy tales have a similar meaning
    D   to add more evidence for Jack Zipes' ideas

40   What does Mathias Clasen believe about fairy tales?

    A   They are a safe way of learning to deal with fear.
    B   They are a type of entertainment that some people avoid.
    C   They reflect the changing values of our society.
    D   They reduce our ability to deal with real-world problems.

WRITING

WRITING TASK 1

You should spend about 20 minutes on this task.

> *The diagram below shows how instant noodles are manufactured.*
>
> *Summarise the information by selecting and reporting the main features, and make comparisons where relevant.*

Write at least 150 words.

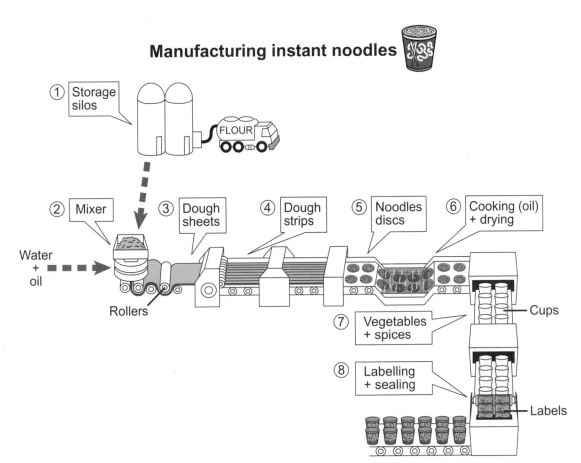

Manufacturing instant noodles

① Storage silos

② Mixer

③ Dough sheets

④ Dough strips

⑤ Noodles discs

⑥ Cooking (oil) + drying

⑦ Vegetables + spices

⑧ Labelling + sealing

Water + oil

Rollers

Cups

Labels

→ p. 133

WRITING TASK 2

You should spend about 40 minutes on this task.

Write about the following topic:

> ***Some people say that advertising is extremely successful at persuading us to buy things. Other people think that advertising is so common that we no longer pay attention to it.***
>
> ***Discuss both these views and give your own opinion.***

Give reasons for your answer and include any relevant examples from your own knowledge or experience.

Write at least 250 words.

SPEAKING

PART 1

The examiner asks the candidate about him/herself, his/her home, work or studies and other familiar topics.

EXAMPLE

Swimming

- Did you learn to swim when you were a child? [Why/Why not?]
- How often do you go swimming now? [Why/Why not?]
- What places are there for swimming where you live? [Why?]
- Do you think it would be more enjoyable to go swimming outdoors or at an indoor pool? [Why?]

PART 2

Describe a famous business person that you know about.

You should say:
  who this person is
  what kind of business this person is involved in
  what you know about this business person

and explain what you think of this business person.

You will have to talk about the topic for one to two minutes. You have one minute to think about what you are going to say. You can make some notes to help you if you wish.

PART 3

Discussion topics:

Famous people today

Example questions:
What kinds of people are most famous in your country today?
Why are there so many stories about famous people in the news?
Do you agree or disagree that many young people today want to be famous?

Advantages of being famous

Example questions:
Do you think it is easy for famous people to earn a lot of money?
Why might famous people enjoy having fans?
In what ways could famous people use their influence to do good things in the world?

Test 4

PART 1   *Questions 1–10*

Complete the form below.

*Write **ONE WORD AND/OR A NUMBER** for each answer.*

Listening test audio

Customer Satisfaction Survey

Customer details

Name: Sophie Bird

Occupation: **1** ....

Reason for travel today: **2** ....

Journey information

Name of station returning to: **3** ....

Type of ticket purchased: standard **4** .... ticket

Cost of ticket: **5** £ ....

When ticket was purchased: yesterday

Where ticket was bought: **6** ....

Satisfaction with journey

Most satisfied with: the wifi

Least satisfied with: the **7** .... this morning

Satisfaction with station facilities

Most satisfied with: how much **8** .... was provided

Least satisfied with: lack of seats, particularly on the **9** ....

Neither satisfied nor dissatisfied with: the **10** .... available

---

PART 2   *Questions 11–20*

Questions 11–16

Label the map below.

*Write the correct letter, **A–H**, next to Questions 11–16.*

Listening test audio

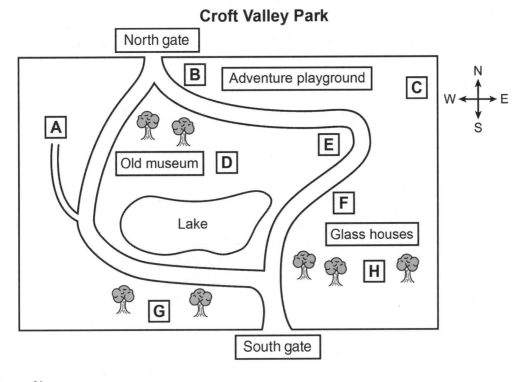

11   café   ....

12   toilets   ....

13   formal gardens   ....

14   outdoor gym   ....

15   skateboard ramp   ....

16   wild flowers   ....

Questions 17 and 18

*Choose **TWO** letters, **A–E**.*

What does the speaker say about the adventure playground?

    A   Children must be supervised.
    B   It costs more in winter.
    C   Some activities are only for younger children.
    D   No payment is required.
    E   It was recently expanded.

Questions 19 and 20

*Choose **TWO** letters, **A–E**.*

What does the speaker say about the glass houses?

    A   They are closed at weekends.
    B   Volunteers are needed to work there.
    C   They were badly damaged by fire.
    D   More money is needed to repair some of the glass.
    E   Visitors can see palm trees from tropical regions.

PART 3   *Questions 21–30*

Questions 21–24

*Choose the correct letter, **A**, **B** or **C**.*

Listening test audio

Presentation about refrigeration

21   What did Annie discover from reading about icehouses?

    A   why they were first created
    B   how the ice was kept frozen
    C   where they were located

22   What point does Annie make about refrigeration in ancient Rome?

    A   It became a commercial business.
    B   It used snow from nearby.
    C   It took a long time to become popular.

23   In connection with modern refrigerators, both Annie and Jack are worried about

    A   the complexity of the technology.
    B   the fact that some are disposed of irresponsibly.
    C   the large number that quickly break down.

24   What do Jack and Annie agree regarding domestic fridges?

    A   They are generally good value for money.
    B   There are plenty of useful variations.
    C   They are more useful than other domestic appliances.

Questions 25–30

Who is going to do research into each topic?

*Write the correct letter, **A**, **B** or **C**, next to Questions 25–30.*

People
A Annie
B Jack
C both Annie and Jack

Topics

25	the goods that are refrigerated	....
26	the effects on health	....
27	the impact on food producers	....
28	the impact on cities	....
29	refrigerated transport	....
30	domestic fridges	....

PART 4   *Questions 31–40*

Complete the notes below.

*Write **ONE WORD ONLY** for each answer.*

Listening test audio

How the Industrial Revolution affected life in Britain

19th century

- For the first time, people's possessions were used to measure Britain's
  31 ....

- Developments in production of goods and in **32** ....
  greatly changed lives.

MAIN AREAS OF CHANGE

Manufacturing

- The Industrial Revolution would not have happened without the new types of
  33 .... that were used then.

- The leading industry was **34** .... (its products became
  widely available).

- New **35** .... made factories necessary and so more
  people moved into towns.

Transport

- The railways took the place of canals.

- Because of the new transport:

  - greater access to **36** .... made people more aware
    of what they could buy in shops.

  - when shopping, people were not limited to buying
    37 ....goods.

Retailing

- The first department stores were opened.

- The displays of goods were more visible:

  - inside stores because of better **38** ....

  - outside stores, because **39** .... were bigger.

- **40** .... that was persuasive became much more common.

→ 🔾 p. 125   📱 p. 117

READING

READING PASSAGE 1

*You should spend about 20 minutes on **Questions 1–13**, which are based on Reading Passage 1 below.*

The return of the huarango

The arid valleys of southern Peru are welcoming the return of a native plant

The south coast of Peru is a narrow, 2,000-kilometre-long strip of desert squeezed between the Andes and the Pacific Ocean. It is also one of the most fragile ecosystems on Earth. It hardly ever rains there, and the only year-round source of water is located tens of metres below the surface. This is why the huarango tree is so suited to life there: it has the longest roots of any tree in the world. They stretch down 50–80 metres and, as well as sucking up water for the tree, they bring it into the higher subsoil, creating a water source for other plant life.

Dr David Beresford-Jones, archaeobotanist at Cambridge University, has been studying the role of the huarango tree in landscape change in the Lower Ica Valley in southern Peru. He believes the huarango was key to the ancient people's diet and, because it could reach deep water sources, it allowed local people to withstand years of drought when their other crops failed. But over the centuries huarango trees were gradually replaced with crops. Cutting down native woodland leads to erosion, as there is nothing to keep the soil in place. So when the huarangos go, the land turns into a desert. Nothing grows at all in the Lower Ica Valley now.

For centuries the huarango tree was vital to the people of the neighbouring Middle Ica Valley too. They grew vegetables under it and ate products made from its seed pods. Its leaves and bark were used for herbal remedies, while its branches were used for charcoal for cooking and heating, and its trunk was used to build houses. But now it is disappearing rapidly. The majority of the huarango forests in the valley have already been cleared for fuel and agriculture – initially, these were smallholdings, but now they're huge farms producing crops for the international market.

'Of the forests that were here 1,000 years ago, 99 per cent have already gone,' says botanist Oliver Whaley from Kew Gardens in London, who, together with ethnobotanist Dr William Milliken, is running a pioneering project to protect and restore the rapidly disappearing habitat. In order to succeed, Whaley needs to get the local people on board, and that has meant overcoming local prejudices. 'Increasingly aspirational communities think that if you plant food trees in your home or street, it shows you are poor, and still need to grow your own food,' he says. In order to stop the Middle Ica Valley going the same way as the Lower Ica Valley, Whaley is encouraging locals to love the huarangos again. 'It's a process of cultural resuscitation,' he says. He has already set up a huarango festival to reinstate a sense of pride in their eco-heritage, and has helped local schoolchildren plant thousands of trees.

'In order to get people interested in habitat restoration, you need to plant a tree that is useful to them,' says Whaley. So, he has been working with local families to attempt to create a sustainable income from the huarangos by turning their products into foodstuffs. 'Boil up the beans and you get this thick brown syrup like molasses. You can also use it in drinks, soups or stews.' The pods can be ground into flour to make cakes, and the seeds roasted into a sweet, chocolatey 'coffee'. 'It's packed full of vitamins and minerals,' Whaley says.

And some farmers are already planting huarangos. Alberto Benevides, owner of Ica Valley's only certified organic farm, which Whaley helped set up, has been planting the tree for 13 years. He produces syrup and flour, and sells these products at an organic farmers' market in Lima. His farm is relatively small and doesn't yet provide him with enough to live on, but he hopes this will change. 'The organic market is growing rapidly in Peru,' Benevides says. 'I am investing in the future.'

But even if Whaley can convince the local people to fall in love with the huarango again, there is still the threat of the larger farms. Some of these cut across the forests and break up the corridors that allow the essential movement of mammals, birds and pollen up and down the narrow forest strip. In the hope of counteracting this, he's persuading farmers to let him plant forest corridors on their land. He believes the extra woodland will also benefit the farms by reducing their water usage through a lowering of evaporation and providing a refuge for bio-control insects.

'If we can record biodiversity and see how it all works, then we're in a good position to move on from there. Desert habitats can reduce down to very little,' Whaley explains. 'It's not like a rainforest that needs to have this huge expanse. Life has always been confined to corridors and islands here. If you just have a few trees left, the population can grow up quickly because it's used to exploiting water when it arrives.' He sees his project as a model that has the potential to be rolled out across other arid areas around the world. 'If we can do it here, in the most fragile system on Earth, then that's a real message of hope for lots of places, including Africa, where there is drought and they just can't afford to wait for rain.'

Test 4

Questions 1–5

Complete the notes below.

Choose **ONE WORD ONLY** from the passage for each answer.

Write your answers in boxes 1–5 on your answer sheet.

The importance of the huarango tree

–   its roots can extend as far as 80 metres into the soil

–   can access **1** .... deep below the surface

–   was a crucial part of local inhabitants' **2** .... a long time ago

–   helped people to survive periods of **3** ....

–   prevents **4** .... of the soil

–   prevents land from becoming a **5** ....

Questions 6–8

Complete the table below.

Choose **NO MORE THAN TWO WORDS** from the passage for each answer.

Write your answers in boxes 6–8 on your answer sheet.

Traditional uses of the huarango tree

Part of tree	Traditional use
6	fuel
7 .... and	medicine
8	construction

Questions 9–13

Do the following statements agree with the information given in Reading Passage 1?

In boxes 9–13 on your answer sheet, write

> **TRUE**   *if the statement agrees with the information*
> **FALSE**   *if the statement contradicts the information*
> **NOT GIVEN**   *if there is no information on this*

9   Local families have told Whaley about some traditional uses of huarango products.

10   Farmer Alberto Benevides is now making a good profit from growing huarangos.

11   Whaley needs the co-operation of farmers to help preserve the area's wildlife.

12   For Whaley's project to succeed, it needs to be extended over a very large area.

13   Whaley has plans to go to Africa to set up a similar project.

READING PASSAGE 2

*You should spend about 20 minutes on **Questions 14–26**, which are based on Reading Passage 2 below.*

Silbo Gomero – the whistle 'language' of the Canary Islands

La Gomera is one of the Canary Islands situated in the Atlantic Ocean off the northwest coast of Africa. This small volcanic island is mountainous, with steep rocky slopes and deep, wooded ravines, rising to 1,487 metres at its highest peak. It is also home to the best known of the world's whistle 'languages', a means of transmitting information over long distances which is perfectly adapted to the extreme terrain of the island.

This 'language', known as 'Silbo' or 'Silbo Gomero' – from the Spanish word for 'whistle' – is now shedding light on the language-processing abilities of the human brain, according to scientists. Researchers say that Silbo activates parts of the brain normally associated with spoken language, suggesting that the brain is remarkably flexible in its ability to interpret sounds as language.

'Science has developed the idea of brain areas that are dedicated to language, and we are starting to understand the scope of signals that can be recognised as language,' says David Corina, co-author of a recent study and associate professor of psychology at the University of Washington in Seattle.

Silbo is a substitute for Spanish, with individual words recoded into whistles which have high- and low-frequency tones. A whistler – or *silbador* – puts a finger in his or her mouth to increase the whistle's pitch, while the other hand can be cupped to adjust the direction of the sound. 'There is much more ambiguity in the whistled signal than in the spoken signal,' explains lead researcher Manuel Carreiras, psychology professor at the University of La Laguna on the Canary island of Tenerife. Because whistled 'words' can be hard to distinguish, silbadores rely on repetition, as well as awareness of context, to make themselves understood.

The silbadores of Gomera are traditionally shepherds and other isolated mountain folk, and their novel means of staying in touch allows them to communicate over distances of up to 10 kilometres. Carreiras explains that silbadores are able to pass a surprising amount of information via their whistles. 'In daily life they use whistles to communicate short commands, but any Spanish sentence could be whistled.' Silbo has proved particularly useful when fires have occurred on the island and rapid communication across large areas has been vital.

The study team used neuroimaging equipment to contrast the brain activity of silbadores while listening to whistled and spoken Spanish. Results showed the left temporal lobe of the brain, which is usually associated with spoken language, was engaged during the processing of Silbo. The researchers found that other key regions in the brain's frontal lobe also responded to the whistles, including those activated in response to sign language among deaf people. When the experiments were repeated with non-whistlers, however, activation was observed in all areas of the brain.

'Our results provide more evidence about the flexibility of human capacity for language in a variety of forms,' Corina says. 'These data suggest that left-hemisphere language regions are uniquely adapted for communicative purposes, independent of the modality of signal. The non-Silbo speakers were not recognising Silbo as a language. They had nothing to grab onto, so multiple areas of their brains were activated.'

Carreiras says the origins of Silbo Gomero remain obscure, but that indigenous Canary Islanders, who were of North African origin, already had a whistled language when Spain conquered the volcanic islands in the 15th century. Whistled languages survive today in Papua New Guinea, Mexico, Vietnam, Guyana, China, Nepal, Senegal, and a few mountainous pockets in southern Europe. There are thought to be as many as 70 whistled languages still in use, though only 12 have been described and studied scientifically. This form of communication is an adaptation found among cultures where people are often isolated from each other, according to Julien Meyer, a researcher at the Institute of Human Sciences in Lyon, France. 'They are mostly used in mountains or dense forests,' he says. 'Whistled languages are quite clearly defined and represent an original adaptation of the spoken language for the needs of isolated human groups.'

But with modern communication technology now widely available, researchers say whistled languages like Silbo are threatened with extinction. With dwindling numbers of Gomera islanders still fluent in the language, Canaries' authorities are taking steps to try to ensure its survival. Since 1999, Silbo Gomero has been taught in all of the island's elementary schools. In addition, locals are seeking assistance from the United Nations Educational, Scientific and Cultural Organization (UNESCO). 'The local authorities are trying to get an award from the organisation to declare [Silbo Gomero] as something that should be preserved for humanity,' Carreiras adds.

Questions 14–19

Do the following statements agree with the information given in Reading Passage 2?

In boxes 14–19 on your answer sheet, write

> **TRUE**   *if the statement agrees with the information*
> **FALSE**   *if the statement contradicts the information*
> **NOT GIVEN**   *if there is no information on this*

14   La Gomera is the most mountainous of all the Canary Islands.

15   Silbo is only appropriate for short and simple messages.

16   In the brain–activity study, silbadores and non-whistlers produced different results.

17   The Spanish introduced Silbo to the islands in the 15th century.

18   There is precise data available regarding all of the whistle languages in existence today.

19   The children of Gomera now learn Silbo.

Questions 20–26

Complete the notes below.

*Choose **ONE WORD ONLY** from the passage for each answer.*

Write your answers in boxes 20–26 on your answer sheet.

Silbo Gomero

How Silbo is produced

- high- and low-frequency tones represent different sounds in Spanish **20** ....

- pitch of whistle is controlled using silbador's **21** ....

- **22** .... is changed with a cupped hand

How Silbo is used

- has long been used by shepherds and people living in secluded locations

- in everyday use for the transmission of brief **23** ....

- can relay essential information quickly, e.g. to inform people about **24** ....

The future of Silbo

- future under threat because of new **25** ....

- Canaries' authorities hoping to receive a UNESCO **26** .... to help preserve it

---

READING PASSAGE 3

*You should spend about 20 minutes on **Questions 27–40**, which are based on Reading Passage 3 below.*

Environmental practices of big businesses

The environmental practices of big businesses are shaped by a fundamental fact that for many of us offends our sense of justice. Depending on the circumstances, a business may maximize the amount of money it makes, at least in the short term, by damaging the environment and hurting people. That is still the case today for fishermen in an unmanaged fishery without quotas, and for international logging companies with short-term leases on tropical rainforest land in places with corrupt officials and unsophisticated landowners. When government regulation is effective, and when the public is environmentally aware, environmentally clean big businesses may out-compete dirty ones, but the reverse is likely to be true if government regulation is ineffective and if the public doesn't care.

It is easy for the rest of us to blame a business for helping itself by hurting other people. But blaming alone is unlikely to produce change. It ignores the fact that businesses are not charities but profit-making companies, and that publicly owned companies with shareholders are under obligation to those shareholders to maximize profits, provided that they do so by legal means. US laws make a company's directors legally liable for something termed 'breach of fiduciary responsibility' if they knowingly manage a company in a way that reduces profits. The car manufacturer Henry Ford was in fact successfully sued by shareholders in 1919 for raising the minimum wage of his workers to $5 per day: the courts declared that, while Ford's humanitarian sentiments about his employees were nice, his business existed to make profits for its stockholders.

Our blaming of businesses also ignores the ultimate responsibility of the public for creating the conditions that let a business profit through destructive environmental policies. In the long run, it is the public, either directly or through its politicians, that has the power to make such destructive policies unprofitable and illegal, and to make sustainable environmental policies profitable.

The public can do that by suing businesses for harming them, as happened after the Exxon Valdez disaster, in which over $40,000 \, \text{m}^3$ of oil were spilled off the coast of Alaska. The public may also make their opinion felt by preferring to buy sustainably harvested products; by making employees of companies with poor track records feel ashamed of their company and complain to their own management; by preferring their governments to award valuable contracts to businesses with a good environmental track record; and by pressing their governments to pass and enforce laws and regulations requiring good environmental practices.

In turn, big businesses can exert powerful pressure on any suppliers that might ignore public or government pressure. For instance, after the US public became concerned about the spread of a disease known as BSE, which was transmitted to humans through infected meat, the US government's Food and Drug Administration introduced rules demanding that the meat industry abandon practices associated with the risk of the disease spreading. But for five years the meat packers refused to follow these, claiming that they would be too expensive to obey. However, when a major fast-food company then made the same demands after customer purchases of its hamburgers plummeted, the meat industry complied within weeks. The public's task is therefore to identify which links in the supply chain are sensitive to public pressure: for instance, fast–food chains or jewelry stores, but not meat packers or gold miners.

Some readers may be disappointed or outraged that I place the ultimate responsibility for business practices harming the public on the public itself. I also believe that the public must accept the necessity for higher prices for products to cover the added costs, if any, of sound environmental practices. My views may seem to ignore the belief that businesses should act in accordance with moral principles even if this leads to a reduction in their profits. But I think we have to recognize that, throughout human history, in all politically complex human societies, government regulation has arisen precisely because it was found that not only did moral principles need to be made explicit, they also needed to be enforced.

To me, the conclusion that the public has the ultimate responsibility for the behavior of even the biggest businesses is empowering and hopeful, rather than disappointing. My conclusion is not a moralistic one about who is right or wrong, admirable or selfish, a good guy or a bad guy. In the past, businesses have changed when the public came to expect and require different behavior, to reward businesses for behavior that the public wanted, and to make things difficult for businesses practicing behaviors that the public didn't want. I predict that in the future, just as in the past, changes in public attitudes will be essential for changes in businesses' environmental practices.

Questions 27–31

*Complete the summary using the list of words, **A–J**, below.*

*Write the correct letter, **A–J**, in boxes 27–31 on your answer sheet.*

Big businesses

Many big businesses today are prepared to harm people and the environment in order to make money, and they appear to have no **27** .... Lack of **28** .... by governments and lack of public **29** .... can lead to environmental problems such as **30** .... or the destruction of **31** ....

A	funding	**B**	trees	**C**	rare species
D	moral standards	**E**	control	**F**	involvement
G	flooding	**H**	overfishing	**I**	worker support

Questions 32–34

*Choose the correct letter, **A**, **B**, **C** or **D**.*

Write the correct letter in boxes 32–34 on your answer sheet.

32   The main idea of the third paragraph is that environmental damage

    A   requires political action if it is to be stopped.
    B   is the result of ignorance on the part of the public.
    C   could be prevented by the action of ordinary people.
    D   can only be stopped by educating business leaders.

33   In the fourth paragraph, the writer describes ways in which the public can

    A   reduce their own individual impact on the environment.
    B   learn more about the impact of business on the environment.
    C   raise awareness of the effects of specific environmental disasters.
    D   influence the environmental policies of businesses and governments.

34   What pressure was exerted by big business in the case of the disease BSE?

    A   Meat packers stopped supplying hamburgers to fast-food chains.
    B   A fast-food company forced their meat suppliers to follow the law.
    C   Meat packers persuaded the government to reduce their expenses.
    D   A fast-food company encouraged the government to introduce legislation.

Questions 35–39

Do the following statements agree with the claims of the writer in Reading Passage 3?

In boxes 35–39 on your answer sheet, write

> **YES** if the statement agrees with the claims of the writer
> **NO** if the statement contradicts the claims of the writer
> **NOT GIVEN** if it is impossible to say what the writer thinks about this

35 The public should be prepared to fund good environmental practices.

36 There is a contrast between the moral principles of different businesses.

37 It is important to make a clear distinction between acceptable and unacceptable behaviour.

38 The public have successfully influenced businesses in the past.

39 In the future, businesses will show more concern for the environment.

Question 40

Choose the correct letter, **A**, **B**, **C** or **D**.

Write the correct letter in box 40 on your answer sheet.

40 What would be the best subheading for this passage?

> **A** Will the world survive the threat caused by big businesses?
> **B** How can big businesses be encouraged to be less driven by profit?
> **C** What environmental dangers are caused by the greed of businesses?
> **D** Are big businesses to blame for the damage they cause the environment?

WRITING TASK 1

You should spend about 20 minutes on this task.

> *The chart below shows what Anthropology graduates from one university did after finishing their undergraduate degree course. The table shows the salaries of the anthropologists in work after five years.*
>
> *Summarise the information by selecting and reporting the main features, and make comparisons where relevant.*

Write at least 150 words.

Destination of Anthropology graduates (from one university)

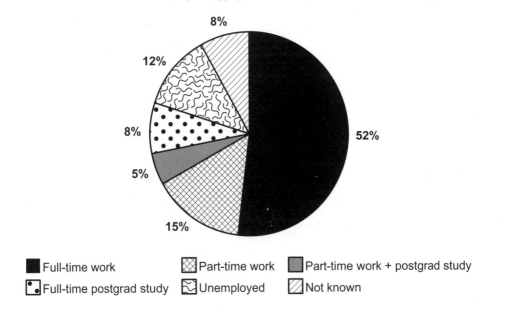

Full-time work   Part-time work   Part-time work + postgrad study
Full-time postgrad study   Unemployed   Not known

Salaries of Antrhropology graduates (after 5 years' work)

Type of employment	$25,000–49,999	$50,000–74,999	$75,000–99,999	$100,000+
Freelance consultants	5%	15%	40%	40%
Government sector	5%	15%	30%	50%
Private companies	10%	35%	25%	30%

→ 🖉 p. 136

WRITING TASK 2

You should spend about 40 minutes on this task.

Write about the following topic:

> *In some cultures, children are often told that they can achieve anything if they try hard enough.*
>
> *What are the advantages and disadvantages of giving children this message?*

Give reasons for your answer and include any relevant examples from your own knowledge or experience.

Write at least 250 words.

SPEAKING

PART 1

The examiner asks the candidate about him/herself, his/her home, work or studies and other familiar topics.

EXAMPLE

Jewellery

- How often do you wear jewellery? [Why/Why not?]
- What type of jewellery do you like best? [Why/Why not?]
- When do people like to give jewellery in your country [Why?]
- Have you ever given jewellery to someone as a gift? [Why/Why not?]

PART 2

> **Describe an interesting TV programme you watched about a science topic.**
>
> **You should say:**
>   **what science topic this TV programme was about**
>   **when you saw this TV programme**
>   **what you learnt from this TV programme about a science topic**
>
> **and explain why you found this TV programme interesting.**

You will have to talk about the topic for one to two minutes. You have one minute to think about what you are going to say. You can make some notes to help you if you wish.

PART 3

Discussion topics:

Science and the public

Example questions:
How interested are most people in your country in science?
Why do you think children today might be better at science than their parents?
How do you suggest the public can learn more about scientific developments?

Scientific discoveries

Example questions:
What do you think are the most important scientific discoveries in the last 100 years?
Do you agree or disagree that there are no more major scientific discoveries left to make?
Who should pay for scientific research – governments or private companies?

Audioscripts

TEST 1

PART 1

AMBER:	Hello William. This is Amber – you said to phone if I wanted to get more information about the job agency you mentioned. Is now a good time?
WILLIAM:	Oh, hi Amber. Yes. Fine. So the agency I was talking about is called Bankside – they're based in Docklands – I can tell you the address now – 497 Eastside.
AMBER:	OK, thanks. So is there anyone in particular I should speak to there?
WILLIAM:	The agent I always deal with is called Becky Jamieson.
AMBER:	Let me write that down – Becky …
WILLIAM:	<u>Jamieson</u> J-A-M-I-E-S-O-N.

Q1

AMBER:	Do you have her direct line?
WILLIAM:	Yes, it's in my contacts somewhere – right, here we are: 078 double 6, 510 triple 3. I wouldn't call her until the <u>afternoon</u> if I were you – she's always really busy in the morning trying to fill last-minute vacancies. She's really helpful and friendly so I'm sure it would be worth getting in touch with her for an informal chat.

Q2

AMBER:	It's mainly clerical and admin jobs they deal with, isn't it?
WILLIAM:	That's right. I know you're hoping to find a full-time job in the media eventually – but Becky mostly recruits temporary staff for the finance sector – which will look good on your CV – and generally pays better too.
AMBER:	Yeah – I'm just a bit worried because I don't have much office experience.
WILLIAM:	I wouldn't worry. They'll probably start you as a receptionist, or something like that. So what's important for that kind of job isn't so much having business skills or knowing lots of different computer systems – it's <u>communication</u> that really matters – so you'd be fine there. And you'll pick up office skills really quickly on the job. It's not that complicated.

Q3

AMBER:	OK good. So how long do people generally need temporary staff for? It would be great if I could get something lasting at least a month.
WILLIAM:	That shouldn't be too difficult. But you're more likely to be offered something for a <u>week</u> at first, which might get extended. It's unusual to be sent somewhere for just a day or two.

Q4

AMBER:	Right. I've heard the pay isn't too bad – better than working in a shop or a restaurant.
WILLIAM:	Oh yes – definitely. The hourly rate is about £<u>10</u>, 11 if you're lucky.

Q5

AMBER:	That's pretty good. I was only expecting to get eight or nine pounds an hour.

WILLIAM:	Do you want me to tell you anything about the registration process?
AMBER:	Yes, please. I know you have to have an interview.
WILLIAM:	The interview usually takes about an hour and you should arrange that about a week in advance.
AMBER:	I suppose I should dress smartly if it's for office work – I can probably borrow a <u>suit</u> from Mum.

Q6

WILLIAM:	Good idea. It's better to look too smart than too casual.
AMBER:	Will I need to bring copies of my exam certificates or anything like that?
WILLIAM:	No – they don't need to see those, I don't think.

AMBER:	What about my <u>passport</u>?	Q7
WILLIAM:	Oh yes – they will ask to see that.	
AMBER:	OK.	
WILLIAM:	I wouldn't get stressed about the interview though. It's just a chance for them to build a relationship with you – so they can try and match you to a job which you'll like. So there are questions about <u>personality</u> that they always ask candidates – fairly basic ones. And they probably won't ask anything too difficult like what your plans are for the future.	Q8
AMBER:	Hope not.	
WILLIAM:	Anyway, there are lots of benefits to using an agency – for example, the interview will be useful because they'll give you <u>feedback</u> on your performance so you can improve next time.	Q9
AMBER:	And they'll have access to jobs which aren't advertised.	
WILLIAM:	Exactly – most temporary jobs aren't advertised.	
AMBER:	And I expect finding a temporary job this way takes a lot less <u>time</u> – it's much easier than ringing up individual companies.	Q10
WILLIAM:	Yes indeed. Well I think …	

PART 2

Good morning. My name's Erica Matthews, and I'm the owner of Matthews Island Holidays, a company set up by my parents. Thank you for coming to this presentation, in which I hope to interest you in what we have to offer. We're a small, family-run company, and we believe in the importance of the personal touch, so we don't aim to compete with other companies on the number of customers. What we do is build on our <u>many years' experience – more than almost any other rail holiday company</u> – to ensure we provide perfect holidays in a small number of destinations, which we've got to know extremely well. [Q11]

I'll start with our six-day Isle of Man holiday. This is a fascinating island in the Irish Sea, with Wales to the south, England to the east, Scotland to the north and Northern Ireland to the west. Our holiday starts in <u>Heysham, where your tour manager will meet you</u>, then you'll travel by ferry to the Isle of Man. Some people prefer to fly from Luton instead, and another popular option is to go by train to Liverpool and take a ferry from there. [Q12]

You have five nights in the hotel, and the price covers five breakfasts and dinners, and <u>lunch on the three days when there are organised trips</u>: day four is free, and most people have lunch in a café or restaurant in Douglas. [Q13]

The price of the holiday includes the ferry to the Isle of Man, all travel on the island, the hotel, and the meals I've mentioned. Incidentally, we try to make booking our holidays as simple and fair as possible, so unlike with many companies, the price is the same whether you book six months in advance or at the last minute, and there's no supplement for single rooms in hotels. <u>If you make a booking then need to change the start date, for example because of illness, you're welcome to change to an alternative date or a different tour, for a small administrative fee</u>. [Q14]

OK, so what does the holiday consist of? Well, on day one you'll arrive in time for a short introduction by your tour manager, followed by dinner in the hotel. The dining room looks out at the <u>river</u>, close to where it flows into the harbour, and there's usually plenty of activity going on. [Q15]

On day two you'll take the coach to the small town of Peel, on the way calling in at the Tynwald Exhibition. The Isle of Man isn't part of the United Kingdom, and it has its own parliament, called Tynwald. It's claimed that this is the world's oldest parliament that's still functioning, and that it dates back to 979. However, the earliest surviving reference to it is from <u>1422</u>, so perhaps it isn't quite as old as it claims! Q16

Day three we have a trip to the mountain Snaefell. This begins with a leisurely ride along the promenade in Douglas in a horse-drawn tram. Then you board an electric train which takes you to the fishing village of Laxey. From there it's an eight-kilometre ride in the Snaefell Mountain Railway to the <u>top</u>. Lunch will be in the café, giving you spectacular views of the island. Q17

Day four is free for you to explore, using the <u>pass</u> which we'll give you. So you won't have to pay for travel on local transport, or for entrance to the island's heritage sites. Or you might just want to take it easy in Douglas and perhaps do a little light shopping. Q18

The last full day, day five, is for some people the highlight of the holiday, with a ride on the <u>steam</u> railway, from Douglas to Port Erin. After some time to explore, a coach will take you to the headland that overlooks the Calf of Man, a small island just off the coast. From there you continue to Castletown, which used to be the <u>capital</u> of the Isle of Man, and its mediaeval castle. Q19 Q20

And on day six it's back to the ferry – or the airport, if you flew to the island – and time to go home.

Now I'd like to tell you ...

PART 3

RUTH:	Ed, how are you getting on with the reading for our presentation next week?
ED:	Well, OK, Ruth – but there's so much of it.
RUTH:	I know, I hadn't realised birth order was such a popular area of research.
ED:	But the stuff on birth order and personality is mostly unreliable. From what I've been reading a lot of the claims about how your position in the family determines certain personality traits are just stereotypes, with no robust evidence to support them.
RUTH:	OK, but that's an interesting point – we could start by outlining what previous research has shown. There are studies going back over a hundred years.
ED:	Yeah – so we could just run through some of the typical traits. Like the consensus seems to be that oldest children are generally less well-adjusted because they never get over the arrival of a younger sibling.
RUTH:	Right, but on a positive note, some studies claimed that <u>they were thought to be good at nurturing – certainly in the past when people had large families they would have been expected to look after the younger ones</u>.
ED:	There isn't such a clear picture for middle children – but one trait that a lot of the studies mention is that they are easier to get on with than older or younger siblings.
RUTH:	<u>Generally eager to please and helpful</u> – although that's certainly not accurate as far as my family goes – my middle brother was a nightmare – always causing fights and envious of whatever I had.
ED:	As I said – none of this seems to relate to my own experience. I'm the youngest in my family and I don't recognise myself in any of the studies I've read about. I'm supposed to have been <u>a sociable and confident child who made friends easily</u> – but I was actually terribly shy.
RUTH:	Really? That's funny. There have been hundreds of studies on twins but mostly about nurture versus nature …

Q21 appears beside the RUTH line "Right, but on a positive note..."
Q22 appears beside the RUTH line "Generally eager to please and helpful..."
Q23 appears beside the ED line "supposed to have been a sociable and confident child..."

ED:	There was one on personality, which said that a twin is likely to be <u>quite shy in social situations</u> because they always have their twin around to depend on for support.	Q24
RUTH:	My cousins were like that when they were small – they were only interested in each other and found it hard to engage with other kids. They're fine now though.	
ED:	Only children have had a really bad press – a lot of studies have branded them as <u>loners who think the world revolves around them</u> because they've never had to fight for their parents' attention.	Q25
RUTH:	That does seem a bit harsh. One category I hadn't considered before was children with much older siblings – a couple of studies mentioned that these children <u>grow up more quickly and are expected to do basic things for themselves – like getting dressed.</u>	Q26
ED:	I can see how that might be true – although I expect they're sometimes the exact opposite – playing the baby role and clamouring for special treatment.	

RUTH:	What was the problem with most of these studies, do you think?	
ED:	I think it was because in a lot of cases data was collected from only one sibling per family, who rated him or herself and his or her siblings at the same time.	
RUTH:	Mmm. Some of the old research into the relationship between birth order and academic achievement has been proved to be accurate though. Performances in intelligence tests decline slightly from the eldest child to his or her younger siblings. This has been proved in lots of recent studies.	
ED:	Yes. <u>Although what many of them didn't take into consideration was family size.</u> The more siblings there are, the likelier the family is to have a low socio-economic status – which can also account for differences between siblings in academic performance.	Q27
RUTH:	The oldest boy might be given more opportunities than his younger sisters, for example.	
ED:	Exactly.	
RUTH:	But the main reason for the marginally higher academic performance of oldest children is quite surprising, I think. It's not only that they benefit intellectually from extra attention at a young age – which is what I would have expected. <u>It's that they benefit from being teachers for their younger siblings, by verbalising processes.</u>	Q28
ED:	Right, and this gives them status and confidence, which again contribute, in a small way, to better performance. So would you say sibling rivalry has been a useful thing for you?	
RUTH:	I think so – my younger brother was incredibly annoying and we fought a lot but I think this has made me a stronger person. <u>I know how to defend myself.</u> We had some terrible arguments and I would have died rather than apologise to him – but <u>we had to put up with each other</u> and most of the time we co-existed amicably enough.	Q29/Q30 Q29/Q30
ED:	Yes, my situation was pretty similar. But I don't think having two older brothers made me any less selfish – I was never prepared to let my brothers use any of my stuff …	
RUTH:	That's perfectly normal, whereas …	

PART 4

Today I'm going to talk about the eucalyptus tree. This is a very common tree here in Australia, where it's also sometimes called the gum tree. First I'm going to talk about why it's important, then I'm going to describe some problems it faces at present.

Right, well the eucalyptus tree is an important tree for lots of reasons. For example, it gives
shelter to creatures like birds and bats, and these and other species also depend on it for   Q31
food, particularly the nectar from its flowers. So it supports biodiversity. It's useful to us
humans too, because we can kill germs with a disinfectant made from oil extracted from   Q32
eucalyptus leaves.

The eucalyptus grows all over Australia and the trees can live for up to four hundred years.
So it's alarming that all across the country, numbers of eucalyptus are falling because the
trees are dying off prematurely. So what are the reasons for this?

One possible reason is disease. As far back as the 1970s the trees started getting a disease
called Mundulla Yellows. The trees' leaves would gradually turn yellow, then the tree would
die. It wasn't until 2004 that they found the cause of the problem was lime, or calcium
hydroxide to give it its proper chemical name, which was being used in the construction
of roads. The lime was being washed away into the ground and affecting the roots of the   Q33
eucalyptus trees nearby. What it was doing was preventing the trees from sucking up the iron
they needed for healthy growth. When this was injected back into the affected trees, they
immediately recovered.

But this problem only affected a relatively small number of trees. By 2000, huge numbers
of eucalyptus were dying along Australia's East Coast, of a disease known as Bell-miner
Associated Die-back. The bell-miner is a bird, and the disease seems to be common where
there are high populations of bell-miners. Again it's the leaves of the trees that are affected.
What happens is that insects settle on the leaves and eat their way round them, destroying   Q34
them as they go, and at the same time they secrete a solution which has sugar in it. The bell-
miner birds really like this solution, and in order to get as much as possible, they keep away
other creatures that might try to get it. So these birds and insects flourish at the expense of
other species, and eventually so much damage is done to the leaves that the tree dies.

But experts say that trees can start looking sick before any sign of Bell-miner Associated Die-
back. So it looks as if the problem might have another explanation. One possibility is that it's
to do with the huge bushfires that we have in Australia. A theory proposed over 40 years ago
by ecologist William Jackson is that the *frequency* of bushfires in a particular region affects
the type of vegetation that grows there. If there are very frequent bushfires in a region, this
encourages grass to grow afterwards, while if the bushfires are rather less frequent, this   Q35
results in the growth of eucalyptus forests.

So why is this? Why do fairly frequent bushfires actually support the growth of eucalyptus?
Well, one reason is that the fire stops the growth of other species which would consume
water needed by eucalyptus trees. And there's another reason. If these other quick-growing   Q36
species of bushes and plants are allowed to proliferate, they harm the eucalyptus in another
way, by affecting the composition of the soil, and removing nutrients from it. So some   Q37
bushfires are actually essential for the eucalyptus to survive as long as they are not too
frequent. In fact there's evidence that Australia's indigenous people practised regular burning
of bush land for thousands of years before the arrival of the Europeans.

But since Europeans arrived on the continent, the number of bushfires has been strictly
controlled. Now scientists believe that this reduced frequency of bushfires to low levels has
led to what's known as 'dry rainforest', which seems an odd name as usually we associate   Q38
tropical rainforest with wet conditions. And what's special about this type of rainforest? Well,
unlike tropical rainforest which is a rich ecosystem, this type of ecosystem is usually a simple   Q39
one. It has very thick, dense vegetation, but not much variety of species. The vegetation
provides lots of shade, so one species that does find it ideal is the bell-miner bird, which
builds its nests in the undergrowth there. But again that's not helpful for the eucalyptus tree.   Q40

TEST 2

PART 1

TIM:	Good morning. You're through to the tourist information office, Tim speaking. How can I help you?	
JEAN:	Oh hello. Could you give me some information about next month's festival, please? My family and I will be staying in the town that week.	
TIM:	Of course. Well it starts with a concert on the afternoon of the 17th.	
JEAN:	Oh I heard about that. The orchestra and singers come from the USA, don't they?	
TIM:	They're from Canada. They're very popular over there. They're going to perform a number of well-known pieces that will appeal to children as well as adults.	
JEAN:	That sounds good. My whole family are interested in music.	
TIM:	The next day, the 18th, there's a performance by a ballet company called <u>Eustatis</u>.	*Q1*
JEAN:	Sorry?	
TIM:	The name is spelt E-U-S-T-A-T-I-S. They appeared in last year's festival, and went down very well. Again, their programme is designed for all ages.	
JEAN:	Good. I expect we'll go to that. I hope there's going to be a play during the festival, a comedy, ideally.	
TIM:	You're in luck! On the 19th and 20th a local amateur group are performing one written by a member of the group. It's called *Jemima*. That'll be on in the town hall. They've already performed it two or three times. I haven't seen it myself, but the <u>review</u> in the local paper was very good.	*Q2*
JEAN:	And is it suitable for children?	
TIM:	Yes, in fact it's aimed more at children than at adults, so both performances are in the afternoon.	
JEAN:	And what about <u>dance</u>? Will there be any performances?	*Q3*
TIM:	Yes, also on the 20th, but in the evening. A professional company is putting on a show of modern pieces, with electronic music by young composers.	
JEAN:	Uh-huh.	
TIM:	The show is about how people communicate, or fail to communicate, with each other, so it's got the rather strange name, <u>*Chat*</u>.	*Q4*
JEAN:	I suppose that's because that's something we do both face to face and online.	
TIM:	That's right.	

TIM:	Now there are also some workshops and other activities. They'll all take place at least once every day, so everyone who wants to take part will have a chance.	
JEAN:	Good. We're particularly interested in cookery – you don't happen to have a cookery workshop, do you?	
TIM:	We certainly do. It's going to focus on how to make food part of a <u>healthy</u> lifestyle, and it'll show that even sweet things like cakes can contain much less sugar than they usually do.	*Q5*
JEAN:	That might be worth going to. We're trying to encourage our children to cook.	
TIM:	Another workshop is just for children, and that's on creating <u>posters</u> to reflect the history of the town. The aim is to make children aware of how both the town and people's lives have changed over the centuries. The results will be exhibited in the community centre. Then the other workshop is in toy-making, and that's for adults only.	*Q6*

JEAN:	Oh, why's that?	
TIM:	Because it involves carpentry – participants will be making toys out of <u>wood</u>, so there'll be a lot of sharp chisels and other tools around.	Q7
JEAN:	It makes sense to keep children away from it.	
TIM:	Exactly. Now let me tell you about some of the outdoor activities. There'll be supervised wild swimming …	
JEAN:	Wild swimming? What's that?	
TIM:	It just means swimming in natural waters, rather than a swimming pool.	
JEAN:	Oh OK. In a <u>lake</u>, for instance.	Q8
TIM:	Yes, there's a beautiful one just outside the town, and that'll be the venue for the swimming. There'll be lifeguards on duty, so it's suitable for all ages. And finally, there'll be a walk in some nearby woods every day. The leader is an expert on <u>insects</u>. He'll show some that live in the woods, and how important they are for the environment. So there are going to be all sorts of different things to do during the festival.	Q9
JEAN:	There certainly are.	
TIM:	If you'd like to read about how the preparations for the festival are going, the festival organiser is keeping a <u>blog</u>. Just search online for the festival website, and you'll find it.	Q10
JEAN:	Well, thank you very much for all the information.	
TIM:	You're welcome. Goodbye.	
JEAN:	Goodbye.	

PART 2

WOMAN:	I'm very pleased to welcome this evening's guest speaker, Mark Logan, who's going to tell us about the recent transformation of Minster Park. Over to you, Mark.	
MARK:	Thank you. I'm sure you're all familiar with Minster Park. It's been a feature of the city for well over a century, and has been the responsibility of the city council for most of that time. What perhaps isn't so well known is the origin of the park: <u>unlike many public parks that started in private ownership, as the garden of a large house, for instance, Minster was some waste land, which people living nearby started planting with flowers in 1892.</u> It was unclear who actually owned the land, and this wasn't settled until 20 years later, when the council took possession of it.	Q11
	You may have noticed the statue near one of the entrances. It's of Diane Gosforth, who played a key role in the history of the park. Once the council had become the legal owner, it planned to sell the land for housing. <u>Many local people</u> wanted it to remain a place that everyone could go to, to enjoy the fresh air and natural environment – remember the park is in a densely populated residential area. <u>Diane Gosforth was one of those people, and she organised petitions and demonstrations</u>, which eventually made the council change its mind about the future of the land.	Q12
	Soon after this the First World War broke out, in 1914, and most of the park was dug up and <u>planted with vegetables</u>, which were sold locally. At one stage the army considered taking it over for troop exercises and got as far as contacting the city council, then decided the park was too small to be of use. There were occasional public meetings during the war, in an area that had been retained as grass.	Q13

After the war, the park was turned back more or less to how it had been before 1914, and continued almost unchanged until recently. Plans for transforming it were drawn up at various times, most recently in 2013, though they were revised in 2015, before any work had started. <u>The changes finally got going in 2016</u>, and were finished on schedule last year.

Q14

OK, let me tell you about some of the changes that have been made – and some things that have been retained. If you look at this map, you'll see the familiar outline of the park, with the river forming the northern boundary, and a gate in each of the other three walls. The statue of Diane Gosforth has been moved: it used to be close to the south gate, but it's now <u>immediately to the north of the lily pond, almost in the centre of the park</u>, which makes it much more visible.

Q15

There's a new area of wooden sculptures, which are <u>on the river bank, where the path from the east gate makes a sharp bend</u>.

Q16

There are two areas that are particularly intended for children. The playground has been enlarged and improved, and that's <u>between the river and the path that leads from the pond to the river</u>.

Q17

Then there's a new maze, a circular series of paths, separated by low hedges. That's <u>near the west gate – you go north from there towards the river and then turn left to reach it</u>.

Q18

There have been tennis courts in the park for many years, and they've been doubled, from four to eight. They're still <u>in the south-west corner of the park, where there's a right-angle bend in the path</u>.

Q19

Something else I'd like to mention is the new fitness area. This is <u>right next to the lily pond on the same side as the west gate</u>.

Q20

Now, as you're all gardeners, I'm sure you'll like to hear about the plants that have been chosen for the park.

PART 3

CATHY:	OK, Graham, so let's check we both know what we're supposed to be doing.
GRAHAM:	OK.
CATHY:	So, for the university's open day, we have to plan a display on British life and literature in the mid-19th century.
GRAHAM:	That's right. But we'll have some people to help us find the materials and set it up, remember – for the moment, we just need to plan it.
CATHY:	Good. So have you gathered who's expected to come and see the display? Is it for the people studying English, or students from other departments? I'm not clear about it.
GRAHAM:	Nor me. That was how it used to be, but it didn't attract many people, so this year it's going to be part of an open day, to raise the university's profile. <u>It'll be publicised in the city, to encourage people to come and find out something of what goes on here.</u> And it's included in the information that's sent to <u>people who are considering applying to study here next year</u>.
CATHY:	Presumably some current students and lecturers will come?
GRAHAM:	I would imagine so, but we've been told to concentrate on the other categories of people.
CATHY:	Right. We don't have to cover the whole range of 19th-century literature, do we?

Q21/Q22

Q21/Q22

GRAHAM:	No, it's entirely up to us. I suggest just using Charles Dickens.	
CATHY:	That's a good idea. <u>Most people have heard of him, and have probably read some of his novels, or seen films based on them</u>, so that's a good lead-in to life in his time.	*Q23/Q24*
GRAHAM:	Exactly. <u>And his novels show the awful conditions that most people had to live in, don't they: he wanted to shock people into doing something about it.</u>	*Q23/Q24*
CATHY:	Did he do any campaigning, other than writing?	
GRAHAM:	Yes, he campaigned for education and other social reforms, and gave talks, but I'm inclined to ignore that and focus on the novels.	
CATHY:	Yes, I agree.	

CATHY:	OK, so now shall we think about a topic linked to each novel?	
GRAHAM:	Yes. I've printed out a list of Dickens's novels in the order they were published, in the hope you'd agree to focus on him!	
CATHY:	You're lucky I *did* agree! Let's have a look. OK, the first was *The Pickwick Papers*, published in 1836. It was very successful when it came out, wasn't it, and was adapted for the theatre straight away.	
GRAHAM:	There's an interesting point, though, that there's <u>a character who keeps falling asleep, and that medical condition was named after the book – Pickwickian Syndrome</u>.	*Q25*
CATHY:	Oh, so why don't we use that as the topic, and include some quotations from the novel?	
GRAHAM:	Right. Next is *Oliver Twist*. There's a lot in the novel about poverty. But maybe something less obvious …	
CATHY:	Well Oliver is taught how to steal, isn't he? We could use that to illustrate the fact that <u>very few children went to school, particularly not poor children, so they learnt in other ways</u>.	*Q26*
GRAHAM:	Good idea. What's next?	
CATHY:	Maybe *Nicholas Nickleby*. Actually he taught in a really cruel school, didn't he?	
GRAHAM:	That's right. But there's also the <u>company of touring actors that Nicholas joins. We could do something on theatres and other amusements of the time</u>. We don't want *only* the bad things, do we?	*Q27*
CATHY:	OK.	
GRAHAM:	What about *Martin Chuzzlewit*? He goes to the USA, doesn't he?	
CATHY:	Yes, and <u>Dickens himself had been there a year before, and drew on his experience there in the novel</u>.	*Q28*
GRAHAM:	I wonder, though … The main theme is selfishness, so we could do something on social justice? No, too general, let's keep to your idea – I think it would work well.	
CATHY:	He wrote *Bleak House* next – that's my favourite of his novels.	
GRAHAM:	Yes, mine too. His satire of the legal system is pretty powerful.	
CATHY:	That's true, but think about Esther, <u>the heroine. As a child she lives with someone she doesn't know is her aunt, who treats her very badly. Then she's very happy living with her guardian, and he puts her in charge of the household. And at the end she gets married and her guardian gives her and her husband a house, where of course they're very happy</u>.	*Q29*
GRAHAM:	Yes, I like that.	
CATHY:	What shall we take next? *Little Dorrit*? Old Mr Dorrit has been in a debtors' prison for years …	
GRAHAM:	So was Dickens's father, wasn't he?	
CATHY:	That's right.	

GRAHAM: What about focusing on <u>the part when Mr Dorrit inherits a fortune, and he starts</u>   *Q30*
           <u>pretending he's always been rich</u>?
CATHY: Good idea.
GRAHAM: OK, so next we need to think about what materials we want to illustrate each
           issue. That's going to be quite hard.

PART 4

I'm going to report on a case study of a programme which has been set up to help rural
populations in Mozambique, a largely agricultural country in South-East Africa.

The programme worked with three communities in Chicualacuala district, near the Limpopo
River. This is a dry and arid region, with unpredictable rainfall. Because of this, people in the
area were unable to support themselves through agriculture and instead they used the forest
as a means of providing themselves with an income, mainly by selling charcoal. However,
this was not a sustainable way of living in the long term, as they were rapidly using up this
resource.

To support agriculture in this dry region, the programme focused primarily on making use of
existing water resources from the Limpopo River by setting up systems of <u>irrigation</u>, which   *Q31*
would provide a dependable water supply for crops and animals. The programme worked
closely with the district government in order to find the best way of implementing this. The
region already had one farmers' association, and it was decided to set up two more of these.
These associations planned and carried out activities including water management, livestock
breeding and agriculture, and it was notable that in general, <u>women</u> formed the majority of   *Q32*
the workforce.

It was decided that in order to keep the crops safe from animals, both wild and domestic,
special areas should be fenced off where the crops could be grown. The community was
responsible for creating these fences, but the programme provided the necessary <u>wire</u> for   *Q33*
making them.

Once the area had been fenced off, it could be cultivated. The land was dug, so that
vegetables and cereals appropriate to the climate could be grown, and the programme
provided the necessary <u>seeds</u> for this. The programme also provided pumps so that water   *Q34*
could be brought from the river in pipes to the fields. However, the labour was all provided by
local people, and they also provided and put up the <u>posts</u> that supported the fences around   *Q35*
the fields.

Once the programme had been set up, its development was monitored carefully. The farmers
were able to grow enough produce not just for their own needs, but also to sell. However,
getting the produce to places where it could be marketed was sometimes a problem, as the
farmers did not have access to <u>transport</u>, and this resulted in large amounts of produce,   *Q36*
especially vegetables, being spoiled. This problem was discussed with the farmers'
associations and it was decided that in order to prevent food from being spoiled, the farmers
needed to learn techniques for its <u>preservation</u>.   *Q37*

There was also an additional initiative that had not been originally planned, but which became a central feature of the programme. This was when farmers started to dig holes for tanks in the fenced-off areas and to fill these with water and use them for breeding <u>fish</u> – an important   Q38
source of protein. After a time, another suggestion was made by local people which hadn't been part of the programme's original proposal, but which was also adopted later on. They decided to try setting up colonies of <u>bees</u>, which would provide honey both for their own   Q39
consumption and to sell.

So what lessons can be learned from this programme? First of all, it tells us that in dry, arid regions, if there is access to a reliable source of water, there is great potential for the development of agriculture. In Chicualacuala, there was a marked improvement in agricultural production, which improved food security and benefited local people by providing them with both food and income. However, it's important to set realistic timelines for each phase of the programme, especially for its <u>design</u>, as mistakes made at this stage may be hard to correct   Q40
later on.

The programme demonstrates that sustainable development is possible in areas where …

TEST 3

PART 1

SALLY:	Good morning. Thanks for coming in to see us here at the agency, Joe. I'm one of the agency representatives, and my name's Sally Baker.
JOE:	Hi Sally. I think we spoke on the phone, didn't we?
SALLY:	That's right, we did. So thank you for sending in your CV. We've had quite a careful look at it and I think we have two jobs that might be suitable for you.
JOE:	OK.
SALLY:	The first one is in a company based in North London. They're looking for an administrative assistant.
JOE:	OK. What sort of company is it?
SALLY:	They're called Home Solutions and they design and make <u>furniture</u>.
JOE:	Oh, I don't know much about that, but it sounds interesting.
SALLY:	Yes, well as I said, they want someone in their office, and looking at your past experience it does look as if you fit quite a few of the requirements. So on your CV it appears you've done some data entry?
JOE:	Yes.
SALLY:	So that's one skill they want. Then they expect the person they appoint to attend <u>meetings</u> and take notes there …
JOE:	OK. I've done that before, yes.
SALLY:	And you'd need to be able to cope with general admin.
JOE:	Filing, and keeping records and so on? That should be OK. And in my last job I also had to manage the <u>diary</u>.
SALLY:	Excellent. That's something they want here too. I'd suggest you add it to your CV – I don't think you mentioned that, did you?
JOE:	No.
SALLY:	So as far as the requirements go, they want good computer skills, of course, and they particularly mention spreadsheets.
JOE:	That should be fine.
SALLY:	And interpersonal skills – which would be something they'd check with your references.
JOE:	I think that should be OK, yes.
SALLY:	Then they mention that they want someone who is careful and takes care with <u>details</u> – just looking at your CV, I'd say you're probably alright there.
JOE:	I think so, yes. Do they want any special experience?
SALLY:	I think they wanted some experience of teleconferencing.
JOE:	I've got three years' experience of that.
SALLY:	Let's see, yes, good. In fact they're only asking for <u>at least one year</u>, so that's great. So is that something that might interest you?
JOE:	It is, yes. The only thing is, you said they were in North London so it would be quite a long commute for me.
SALLY:	OK.

Q1
Q2
Q3
Q4
Q5

SALLY:	So the second position might suit you better as far as the location goes; that's for a warehouse assistant and that's in South London.
JOE:	Yes, that would be a lot closer.
SALLY:	And you've worked in a warehouse before, haven't you?
JOE:	Yes.

SALLY:	So as far as the responsibilities for this position go, they want someone who can manage the stock, obviously, and also <u>deliveries</u>.	Q6
JOE:	That should be OK. You've got to keep track of stuff, but I've always been quite good with numbers.	
SALLY:	Good. that's their first requirement. And they want someone who's computer literate, which we know you are.	
JOE:	Sure.	
SALLY:	Then they mention organisational skills. They want someone who's well organised.	
JOE:	Yes, I think I am.	
SALLY:	And <u>tidy</u>?	Q7
JOE:	Yes, they go together really, don't they?	
SALLY:	Sure. Then the usual stuff; they want someone who can communicate well both orally and in writing.	
JOE:	OK. And for the last warehouse job I had, one of the things I enjoyed most was being part of a <u>team</u>. I found that was really essential for the job.	Q8
SALLY:	Excellent. Yes, they do mention that they want someone who's used to that, yes. Now when you were working in a warehouse last time, what sorts of items were you dealing with?	
JOE:	It was mostly bathroom and kitchen equipment, sinks and stoves and fridges.	
SALLY:	So you're OK moving <u>heavy</u> things?	Q9
JOE:	Sure. I'm quite strong, and I've had the training.	
SALLY:	Good. Now as far as experience goes, they mention they want someone with a licence, and that you have experience of driving in London – so you can cope with the traffic and so on.	
JOE:	Yes, no problem.	
SALLY:	And you've got experience of warehouse work … and the final thing they mention is <u>customer</u> service. I think looking at your CV you're OK there.	Q10
JOE:	Right. So what about pay? Can you tell me a bit more about that, please …	

PART 2

PRESENTER:	My guest on the show today is Alice Riches who started the Street Play Scheme where she lives in Beechwood Road. For those of you that don't already know – Street Play involves local residents closing off their street for a few hours so that children have a chance to play in the street safely. She started it in her own street, Beechwood Road, and the idea caught on, and there are now Street Play Schemes all over the city. So when did you actually start the scheme, Alice?	
ALICE:	Well, I first had the idea when my oldest child was still a toddler, so that's about six years ago now – but it took at least two years of campaigning before we were actually able to make it happen. <u>So the scheme's been up and running for three years now</u>. We'd love to be able to close our road for longer – for the whole weekend, from Saturday morning until Sunday evening, for example. <u>At the moment it's just once a week</u>. But when we started it was only once a month. But we're working on it.	Q11 Q12
PRESENTER:	So what actually happens when Beechwood Road is closed?	
ALICE:	We have <u>volunteer wardens, mostly parents but some elderly residents too, who block off our road at either end</u>. The council have provided special signs but there's always a volunteer there to explain what's happening to any motorists. Generally, they're fine about it – we've only had to get the police involved once or twice.	Q13

Now I should explain that the road isn't completely closed to cars. But only residents' cars are allowed. If people really need to get in or out of Beechwood Road, it's not a problem – <u>as long as they drive at under 20 kilometres per hour.</u> But most people just decide not to use their cars during this time, or they park in another street. The wardens are only there to stop through traffic.

Q14

PRESENTER: So can anyone apply to get involved in Street Play?

ALICE: Absolutely – we want to include all kids <u>in the city – especially those who live on busy roads.</u> It's here that demand is greatest. Obviously, there isn't such demand in wealthier areas where the children have access to parks or large gardens – or in the suburbs where there are usually more places for children to play outside.

Q15

I'd recommend that anyone listening who likes the idea should just give it a go. We've been surprised by the positive reaction of residents all over the city. And that's not just parents. There are always a few who complain but they're a tiny minority. On the whole everyone is very supportive and say <u>they're very happy to see children out on the street</u> – even if it does get quite noisy.

Q16

ALICE: There have been so many benefits of Street Play for the kids. Parents really like the fact that the kids are getting fresh air instead of sitting staring at a computer screen, even if they're not doing anything particularly energetic. And of course it's great that kids can play with their friends outside without being supervised by their parents – but for me the biggest advantage is that kids <u>develop confidence in themselves to be outside without their parents.</u> The other really fantastic thing is that children <u>get to know the adults in the street – it's like having a big extended family.</u>

Q17/Q18
Q17/Q18

PRESENTER: It certainly does have a lot of benefits. I want to move on now and ask you about a related project in King Street.

ALICE: Right. Well this was an experiment I was involved in where local residents decided to try and reduce the traffic along King Street, which is the busiest main road in our area, by persuading people not to use their cars for one day. We thought about making people pay more for parking – but we decided that would be really unpopular – so instead we just stopped people from parking on King Street but left the other car parks open.

It was surprising how much of a difference all this made. As we'd predicted, air quality was significantly better but what I hadn't expected was <u>how much quieter it would be</u> – even with the buses still running. Of course everyone said they felt safer but we were actually amazed that <u>sales in the shops went up considerably that day</u> – we thought there'd be fewer people out shopping – not more.

Q19/Q20

Q19/Q20

PRESENTER: That's really interesting so the fact that …

PART 3

HAZEL: Tom, could I ask you for some advice, please?

TOM: Yes of course, if you think I can help. What's it about?

HAZEL: It's my first media studies assignment, and I'm not sure how to go about it. You must have done it last year.

TOM: Is that the one comparing the coverage of a particular story in a range of newspapers?

HAZEL: That's right.

TOM: Oh yes, I really enjoyed writing it.

HAZEL: So what sort of things do I need to compare?

TOM: Well, there are several things. For example, there's the question of which <u>page</u> of the newspaper the item appears on.

Q21

HAZEL:	You mean, because there's a big difference between having it on the front page and the bottom of page ten, for instance?
TOM:	Exactly. And that shows how important the editor thinks the story is. Then there's the <u>size</u> – how many column inches the story is given, how many columns it spreads over.

Q22

HAZEL:	And I suppose that includes the headline.
TOM:	It certainly does. It's all part of attracting the reader's attention.
HAZEL:	What about <u>graphics</u> – whether there's anything visual in addition to the text?

Q23

TOM:	Yes, you need to consider those, too, because they can have a big effect on the reader's understanding of the story – sometimes a bigger effect than the text itself. Then you'll need to look at how the item is put together: what <u>structure</u> is it given? Bear in mind that not many people read beyond the first paragraph, so what has the journalist put at the beginning? And if, say, there are conflicting opinions about something, does one appear near the end, where people probably won't read it?

Q24

HAZEL:	And newspapers sometimes give wrong or misleading information, don't they? Either deliberately or by accident. Should I be looking at that, too?
TOM:	Yes, if you can. Compare what's in different versions, and as far as possible, try and work out what's true and what isn't. And that relates to a very important point: what's the writer's <u>purpose</u>, or at least the most important one, if they have several. It may seem to be to inform the public, but often it's that they want to create fear, or controversy, or to make somebody look ridiculous.

Q25

HAZEL:	Gosh, I see what you mean. And I suppose the writer may make <u>assumptions</u> about the reader.

Q26

TOM:	That's right – about their knowledge of the subject, their attitudes, and their level of education, which means writing so that the readers understand without feeling patronised. All of that will make a difference to how the story is presented.

HAZEL:	Does it matter what type of story I write about?
TOM:	No – national or international politics, the arts ... Anything, as long as it's covered in two or three newspapers. Though of course it'll be easier and more fun if it's something you're interested in and know something about.
HAZEL:	And on that basis <u>a national news item would be worth analysing – I'm quite keen on politics, so I'll try and find a suitable topic</u>. What did you choose for your analysis, Tom?

Q27

TOM:	I was interested in how newspapers express their opinions explicitly, so <u>I wanted to compare editorials in different papers, but when I started looking, I couldn't find two on the same topic</u> that I felt like analysing.

Q28

HAZEL:	In that case, <u>I won't even bother to look</u>.
TOM:	So in the end I chose a human interest story – a terribly emotional story about a young girl who was very ill, and lots of other people – mostly strangers – raised money so she could go abroad for treatment. Actually, I was surprised – some papers just wrote about how wonderful everyone was, but others considered the broader picture, like why treatment wasn't available here.
HAZEL:	Hmm, <u>I usually find stories like that raise quite strong feelings in me! I'll avoid that. Perhaps I'll choose an arts topic</u>, like different reviews of a film, or something about funding for the arts – I'll think about that.

Q29
Q30

TOM:	Yes, that might be interesting.
HAZEL:	OK, well thanks a lot for your help, Tom. It's been really useful.
TOM:	You're welcome. Good luck with the assignment, Hazel.

PART 4

Nowadays, we use *different* products for personal cleanliness, laundry, dishwashing and household cleaning, but this is very much a 20th-century development.

The origins of cleanliness date back to prehistoric times. Since water is essential for life, the earliest people lived near water and knew something about its cleansing properties – at least that it rinsed mud off their hands.

Q31

During the excavation of ancient Babylon, evidence was found that soapmaking was known as early as 2800 BC. Archaeologists discovered cylinders made of clay, with inscriptions on them saying that fats were boiled with ashes. This is a method of making soap, though there's no reference to the purpose of this material.

Q32

The early Greeks bathed for aesthetic reasons and apparently didn't use soap. Instead, they cleaned their bodies with blocks of sand, pumice and ashes, then anointed themselves with oil, and scraped off the oil and dirt with a metal instrument known as a strigil. They also used oil mixed with ashes. Clothes were washed without soap in streams.

Q33

The ancient Germans and Gauls are also credited with discovering how to make a substance called 'soap', made of melted animal fat and ashes. They used this mixture to tint their hair red.

Q34

Soap got its name, according to an ancient Roman legend, from Mount Sapo, where animals were sacrificed, leaving deposits of animal fat. Rain washed these deposits, along with wood ashes, down into the clay soil along the River Tiber. Women found that this mixture greatly reduced the effort required to wash their clothes.

As Roman civilisation advanced, so did bathing. The first of the famous Roman baths, supplied with water from their aqueducts, was built about 312 BC. The baths were luxurious, and bathing became very popular. And by the second century AD, the Greek physician Galen recommended soap for both medicinal and cleansing purposes.

Q35

After the fall of Rome in 467 AD and the resulting decline in bathing habits, much of Europe felt the impact of filth on public health. This lack of personal cleanliness and related unsanitary living conditions were major factors in the outbreaks of disease in the Middle Ages, and especially the Black Death of the 14th century.

Q36

Nevertheless, soapmaking became an established craft in Europe, and associations of soapmakers guarded their trade secrets closely. Vegetable and animal oils were used with ashes of plants, along with perfume, apparently for the first time. Gradually more varieties of soap became available for shaving and shampooing, as well as bathing and laundering.

Q37

A major step toward large-scale commercial soapmaking occurred in 1791, when a French chemist, Nicholas Leblanc, patented a process for turning salt into soda ash, or sodium carbonate. Soda ash is the alkali obtained from ashes that combines with fat to form soap. The Leblanc process yielded quantities of good-quality, inexpensive soda ash.

Q38

Modern soapmaking was born some 20 years later, in the early 19th century, with the discovery by Michel Eugène Chevreul, another French chemist, of the chemical nature and relationship of fats, glycerine and fatty acids. His studies established the basis for both fat and soap chemistry, and soapmaking became a science. Further developments during the 19th century made it easier and cheaper to manufacture soap.

Q39

Until the 19th century, soap was regarded as a luxury item, and was heavily taxed in several countries. As it became more readily available, it became an everyday necessity, a development that was reinforced <u>when the high tax was removed</u>. Soap was then something ordinary people could afford, and cleanliness standards improved.

Q40

With this widespread use came the development of milder soaps for bathing and soaps for use in the washing machines that were available to consumers by the turn of the 20th century.

TEST 4

PART 1

MAN:	Hello. Do you mind if I ask you some questions about your journey today? We're doing a customer satisfaction survey.
SOPHIE:	Yes. OK. I've got about ten minutes before my train home leaves. I'm on a day trip.
MAN:	Great. Thank you. So first of all, could you tell me your name?
SOPHIE:	It's Sophie Bird.
MAN:	Thank you. And would you mind telling me what you do?
SOPHIE:	I'm a journalist.
MAN:	Oh really? That must be interesting.
SOPHIE:	Yes. It is.
MAN:	So was the reason for your visit here today work?
SOPHIE:	Actually, it's my day off. I came here to do some shopping.
MAN:	Oh right.
SOPHIE:	But I do sometimes come here for work.
MAN:	OK. Now I'd like to ask some questions about your journey today, if that's OK.
SOPHIE:	Yes. No problem.
MAN:	Right, so can you tell me which station you're travelling back to?
SOPHIE:	Staunfirth, where I live.
MAN:	Can I just check the spelling? S-T-A-U-N-F-I-R-T-H?
SOPHIE:	That's right.
MAN:	And you travelled from there this morning?
SOPHIE:	Yes.
MAN:	OK, good. Next, can I ask what kind of ticket you bought? I assume it wasn't a season ticket, as you don't travel every day.
SOPHIE:	That's right. No, I just got a normal return ticket. I don't have a rail card so I didn't get any discount. I keep meaning to get one because it's a lot cheaper.
MAN:	Yes – you'd have saved 20% on your ticket today. So you paid the full price for your ticket?
SOPHIE:	I paid £23.70.
MAN:	OK. Do you think that's good value for money?
SOPHIE:	Not really. I think it's too much for a journey that only takes 45 minutes.
MAN:	Yes, that's one of the main complaints we get. So, you didn't buy your ticket in advance?
SOPHIE:	No. I know it's cheaper if you buy a week in advance but I didn't know I was coming then.
MAN:	I know. You can't always plan ahead. So, did you buy it this morning?
SOPHIE:	No, it was yesterday.
MAN:	Right. And do you usually buy your tickets at the station?
SOPHIE:	Well, I do usually but the ticket office closes early and I hate using ticket machines. I think ticket offices should be open for longer hours. There's always a queue for the machines and they're often out of order.
MAN:	A lot of customers are saying the same thing.
SOPHIE:	So to answer your question … I got an e-ticket online.

Q1
Q2
Q3
Q4
Q5
Q6

MAN:	OK. Thank you. Now I'd like to ask you about your satisfaction with your journey. So what would you say you were most satisfied with today?

SOPHIE:	Well, I like the wifi on the train. It's improved a lot. It makes it easier for me to work if I want to.
MAN:	That's the first time today anyone's mentioned that. It's good to get some positive feedback on that.
SOPHIE:	Mmm.
MAN:	And, is there anything you weren't satisfied with?
SOPHIE:	Well, normally, the trains run on time and are pretty reliable but today there was a <u>delay</u>; the train was about 15 minutes behind schedule.
MAN:	OK. I'll put that down. Now I'd also like to ask about the facilities at this station. You've probably noticed that the whole station's been upgraded. What are you most satisfied with?
SOPHIE:	I think the best thing is that they've improved the amount of <u>information</u> about train times etc. that's given to passengers – it's much clearer – before there was only one board and I couldn't always see it properly – which was frustrating.
MAN:	That's good. And is there anything you're not satisfied with?
SOPHIE:	Let's see … I think things have generally improved a lot. The trains are much more modern and I like the new café. But one thing is that there aren't enough places to sit down, especially on the <u>platforms</u>.
MAN:	OK – so I'll put 'seating' down, shall I, as the thing you're least satisfied with?
SOPHIE:	Yes. OK.
MAN:	Can I ask your opinion about some of the other facilities? We'd like feedback on whether people are satisfied, dissatisfied or neither satisfied nor dissatisfied.
SOPHIE:	OK.
MAN:	What about the <u>parking</u> at the station?
SOPHIE:	Well to be honest, I don't really have an opinion as I never use it.
MAN:	So, neither satisfied nor dissatisfied for that then.
SOPHIE:	Yes, I suppose so …
MAN:	OK, and what about …?

The Q labels on the right: Q7 (aligns with delay), Q8 (information), Q9 (platforms), Q10 (parking)

PART 2

As chair of the town council subcommittee on park facilities, I'd like to bring you up to date on some of the changes that have been made recently to the Croft Valley Park. So if you could just take a look at the map I handed out, let's begin with a general overview. So the basic arrangement of the park hasn't changed – it still has two gates, north and south, and a lake in the middle.

The café continues to serve an assortment of drinks and snacks and is still in the same place, <u>looking out over the lake and next to the old museum</u>.   Q11

We're hoping to change the location of the toilets, and bring them nearer to the centre of the park as they're a bit out of the way at present, <u>near the adventure playground, in the corner of</u>   Q12
<u>your map</u>.

The formal gardens have been replanted and should be at their best in a month or two. They used to be behind the old museum, but we've now used <u>the space near the south gate –</u>   Q13
<u>between the park boundary and the path that goes past the lake towards the old museum</u>.

 We have a new outdoor gym for adults and children, which is already proving very popular. It's <u>by the glass houses, just to the right of the path from the south gate. You have to look for</u>   Q14
<u>it as it's a bit hidden in the trees</u>.

One very successful introduction has been our skateboard ramp. It's in constant use during the evenings and holidays. It's <u>near the old museum, at the end of a little path that leads off</u> <u>from the main path between the lake and the museum.</u>

Q15

We've also introduced a new area for wild flowers, to attract bees and butterflies. It's <u>on</u> <u>a bend in the path that goes round the east side of the lake, just south of the adventure</u> <u>playground.</u>

Q16

Now let me tell you a bit more about some of the changes to Croft Valley Park.

One of our most exciting developments has been the adventure playground. We were aware that we had nowhere for children to let off steam, and decided to use our available funds to set up a completely new facility in a large space to the north of the park. It's open year-round, though it closes early in the winter months, and <u>entrance is completely free</u>. Children can choose whatever activities they want to do, irrespective of their age, but <u>we do ask adults not</u> <u>to leave them on their own there</u>. There are plenty of seats where parents can relax and keep an eye on their children at the same time.

Q17/Q18
Q17/Q18

Lastly, the glass houses. A huge amount of work has been done on them to repair the <u>damage following the disastrous fire that recently destroyed their western side</u>. Over £80,000 was spent on replacing the glass walls and the metal supports, as well as the plants that had been destroyed, although unfortunately the collection of tropical palm trees has proved too expensive to replace up to now. At present the glass houses are open from 10am to 3pm <u>Mondays to Thursdays, and it's hoped to extend this to the weekend soon.</u> We're grateful to all those who helped us by contributing their time and money to this achievement.

Q19/Q20

Q19/Q20

The gardens have …

PART 3

ANNIE:	OK, Jack. Before we plan our presentation about refrigeration, let's discuss what we've discovered so far.	
JACK:	Fine, Annie. Though I have to admit I haven't done much research yet.	
ANNIE:	Nor me. But I found an interesting article about icehouses. I'd seen some 18th- and 19th-century ones here in the UK, so I knew they were often built in a shady area or underground, close to lakes that might freeze in the winter. Then blocks of ice could be cut and stored in the icehouse. But <u>I didn't realise that insulating the blocks with straw or sawdust meant they didn't melt for months.</u> The ancient Romans had refrigeration, too.	Q21
JACK:	I didn't know that.	
ANNIE:	Yes, pits were dug in the ground, and snow was imported from the mountains – even though they were at quite a distance. The snow was stored in the pits. Ice formed at the bottom of it. <u>Both the ice and the snow were then sold.</u> The ice cost more than the snow and my guess is that only the wealthy members of society could afford it.	Q22
JACK:	I wouldn't be surprised. I also came across an article about modern domestic fridges. Several different technologies are used, but they were too complex for me to understand.	
ANNIE:	You have to wonder what happens when people get rid of old ones.	
JACK:	You mean because the gases in them are harmful for the environment?	

ANNIE:	Exactly. At least there are now plenty of organisations that will recycle most of the components safely, but of course <u>some people just dump old fridges in the countryside</u>.
JACK:	<u>It's hard to see how they can be stopped unfortunately</u>. In the UK we get rid of three million a year altogether!
ANNIE:	That sounds a lot, especially because fridges hardly ever break down.
JACK:	That's right. In this country we keep domestic fridges for 11 years on average, and a lot last for 20 or more. So <u>if you divide the cost by the number of years you can use a fridge, they're not expensive, compared with some household appliances</u>.
ANNIE:	<u>True</u>. I suppose manufacturers encourage people to spend more by making them different colours and designs. I'm sure when my parents bought their first fridge they had hardly any choice!
JACK:	Yes, there's been quite a change.

Q23

Q24

JACK:	Right, let's make a list of topics to cover in our presentation, and decide who's going to do more research on them. Then later, we can get together and plan the next step.
ANNIE:	OK. How about starting with how useful refrigeration is, and <u>the range of goods that are refrigerated</u> nowadays? Because of course it's not just food and drinks.
JACK:	No, I suppose flowers and medicines are refrigerated, too.
ANNIE:	And computers. <u>I could do that</u>, unless you particularly want to.
JACK:	No, that's fine by me. What about <u>the effects of refrigeration on people's health</u>? After all, some of the chemicals used in the 19th century were pretty harmful, but there have been lots of benefits too, like always having access to fresh food. Do you fancy dealing with that?
ANNIE:	I'm not terribly keen, to be honest.
JACK:	Nor me. My mind just goes blank when I read anything about chemicals.
ANNIE:	<u>Oh, all right then, I'll do you a favour</u>. But you owe me, Jack. OK. What about <u>the effects on food producers</u>, like farmers in poorer countries being able to export their produce to developed countries? Something for you, maybe?
JACK:	<u>I don't mind</u>. It should be quite interesting.
ANNIE:	I think we should also look at <u>how refrigeration has helped whole cities</u> – like Las Vegas, which couldn't exist without refrigeration because it's in the middle of a desert.
JACK:	Right. I had a quick look at an economics book in the library that's got a chapter about this sort of thing. I could give you the title, if you want to do this section.
ANNIE:	Not particularly, to be honest. I find economics books pretty heavy going, as a rule.
JACK:	<u>OK, leave it to me, then</u>.
ANNIE:	Thanks. Then there's transport, and the difference that <u>refrigerated trucks</u> have made. <u>I wouldn't mind having a go at that</u>.
JACK:	Don't forget trains, too. I read something about milk and butter being transported in refrigerated railroad cars in the USA, right back in the 1840s.
ANNIE:	I hadn't thought of trains. Thanks.
JACK:	Shall we have a separate section on <u>domestic fridges</u>? After all, they're something everyone's familiar with.

Q25

Q26

Q27

Q28

Q29

Q30

ANNIE: <u>What about splitting it into two</u>? You could investigate 19th- and 20th-century fridges, and I'll concentrate on what's available these days, and how manufacturers differentiate their products from those of their competitors.

JACK: <u>OK, that'd suit me</u>.

PART 4

Hi everyone, in this session I'll be presenting my research about the social history of Britain during the Industrial Revolution. I particularly looked at how ordinary lives were affected by changes that happened at that time. This was a time that saw the beginning of a new phenomenon: consumerism – where buying and selling goods became a major part of ordinary people's lives.

In fact, it was in the 19th century that the quantity and quality of people's possessions was used as an indication of the <u>wealth</u> of the country. Before this, the vast majority of people had very few possessions, but all that was changed by the Industrial Revolution. This was the era from the mid-18th to the late 19th century, when improvements in how goods were made as well as in <u>technology</u> triggered massive social changes that transformed life for just about everybody in several key areas.

Q31

Q32

First let's look at manufacturing. When it comes to manufacturing, we tend to think of the Industrial Revolution in images of steam engines and coal. And it's true that the Industrial Revolution couldn't have taken place at all if it weren't for these new sources of <u>power</u>. They marked an important shift away from the traditional watermills and windmills that had dominated before this. The most advanced industry for much of the 19th century was <u>textiles</u>. This meant that fashionable fabrics, and lace and ribbons were made available to everyone.

Q33

Q34

Before the Industrial Revolution, most people made goods to sell in small workshops, often in their own homes. But enormous new <u>machines</u> were now being created that could produce the goods faster and on a larger scale, and these required a lot more space. So large factories were built, replacing the workshops, and forcing workers to travel to work. In fact, large numbers of people migrated from villages into towns as a result.

Q35

As well as manufacturing, there were new technologies in transport, contributing to the growth of consumerism. The horse-drawn stagecoaches and carts of the 18th century, which carried very few people and goods, and travelled slowly along poorly surfaced roads, were gradually replaced by the numerous canals that were constructed. These were particularly important for the transportation of goods. The canals gradually fell out of use, though, as railways were developed, becoming the main way of moving goods and people from one end of the country to the other. And the goods they moved weren't just coal, iron, clothes, and so on – significantly, they included <u>newspapers</u>, which meant that thousands of people were not only more knowledgeable about what was going on in the country, but could also read about what was available in the shops. And that encouraged them to buy more. So faster forms of transport resulted in distribution becoming far more efficient – goods could now be sold all over the country, instead of just in the <u>local</u> market.

Q36

Q37

The third main area that saw changes that contributed to consumerism was retailing. The number and quality of shops grew rapidly, and in particular, small shops suffered as customers flocked to the growing number of department stores – a form of retailing that was new in the 19th century. The entrepreneurs who opened these found new ways to stock them with goods, and to attract customers: for instance, improved <u>lighting</u> inside greatly increased the visibility of the goods for sale. Another development that made goods more visible from outside resulted from the use of plate glass, which made it possible for <u>windows</u> to be much larger than previously. New ways of promoting goods were introduced, too. Previously, the focus had been on *informing* potential customers about the availability of goods; now there was an explosion in <u>advertising</u> trying to persuade people to go shopping.

Q38

Q39

Q40

Flanders claims that one of the great effects of the Industrial Revolution was that it created choice. All sorts of things that had previously been luxuries – from sugar to cutlery – became conveniences, and before long they'd turned into necessities: life without sugar or cutlery was unimaginable. Rather like mobile phones these days!

Listening and Reading answer keys

TEST 1

LISTENING

 Answer key with extra explanations in Resource bank

Part 1, Questions 1–10

1 Jamieson
2 afternoon
3 communication
4 week
5 10/ten
6 suit
7 passport
8 personality
9 feedback
10 time

Part 3, Questions 21–30

21 G
22 F
23 A
24 E
25 B
26 C
27 C
28 A
29&30 *IN EITHER ORDER*
   B
   D

Part 2, Questions 11–20

11 A
12 B
13 A
14 C
15 river
16 1422
17 top
18 pass
19 steam
20 capital

Part 4, Questions 31–40

31 shelter
32 oil
33 roads
34 insects
35 grass(es)
36 water
37 soil
38 dry
39 simple
40 nest(s)

If you score …

0–17	18–27	28–40
you are unlikely to get an acceptable score under examination conditions and we recommend that you spend a lot of time improving your English before you take IELTS.	you may get an acceptable score under examination conditions but we recommend that you think about having more practice or lessons before you take IELTS.	you are likely to get an acceptable score under examination conditions but remember that different institutions will find different scores acceptable.

TEST 1

READING

 Answer key with extra explanations in Resource bank

Reading Passage 1, Questions 1–13

1 oval
2 husk
3 seed
4 mace
5 FALSE
6 NOT GIVEN
7 TRUE
8 Arabs
9 plague
10 lime
11 Run
12 Mauritius
13 tsunami

Reading Passage 2, Questions 14–26

14 C
15 B
16 E
17 G
18 D
19 human error
20 car (-) sharing
21 ownership
22 mileage
23&24 *IN EITHER ORDER*
    C
    D
25&26 *IN EITHER ORDER*
    A
    E

Reading Passage 3, Questions 27–40

27 A
28 C
29 C
30 D
31 A
32 B
33 E
34 A
35 D
36 E
37 B
38 (unique) expeditions
39 uncontacted / isolated
40 (land) surface

If you score ...

0–15	16–24	25–40
you are unlikely to get an acceptable score under examination conditions and we recommend that you spend a lot of time improving your English before you take IELTS.	you may get an acceptable score under examination conditions but we recommend that you think about having more practice or lessons before you take IELTS.	you are likely to get an acceptable score under examination conditions but remember that different institutions will find different scores acceptable.

TEST 2

LISTENING

 Answer key with extra explanations in Resource bank

Part 1, Questions 1–10

1   Eustatis
2   review
3   dance
4   *Chat*
5   healthy
6   posters
7   wood
8   lake
9   insects
10 blog

Part 2, Questions 11–20

11 C
12 A
13 B
14 C
15 E
16 C
17 B
18 A
19 G
20 D

Part 3, Questions 21–30

21&22 *IN EITHER ORDER*
      B
      D
23&24 *IN EITHER ORDER*
      B
      C
25 G
26 B
27 D
28 C
29 H
30 F

Part 4, Questions 31–40

31 irrigation
32 women
33 wire(s)
34 seed(s)
35 posts
36 transport
37 preservation
38 fish(es)
39 bees
40 design

If you score …

0–18	19–27	28–40
you are unlikely to get an acceptable score under examination conditions and we recommend that you spend a lot of time improving your English before you take IELTS.	you may get an acceptable score under examination conditions but we recommend that you think about having more practice or lessons before you take IELTS.	you are likely to get an acceptable score under examination conditions but remember that different institutions will find different scores acceptable.

TEST 2

READING

 Answer key with extra explanations in Resource bank

Reading Passage 1, Questions 1–13

1   B
2   C
3   F
4   D
5   E
6   A
7   safety
8   traffic
9   carriageway
10   mobile
11   dangerous
12   communities
13   healthy

Reading Passage 2, Questions 14–26

14   F
15   A
16   D
17   A
18   genetic traits
19   heat loss
20   ears
21   (insulating) fat
22   (carbon) emissions
23   B
24   C
25   A
26   C

Reading Passage 3, Questions 27–40

27   C
28   A
29   B
30   B
31   D
32   F
33   H
34   C
35   D
36   E
37   NOT GIVEN
38   YES
39   NO
40   NO

If you score …

0–15	16–25	26–40
you are unlikely to get an acceptable score under examination conditions and we recommend that you spend a lot of time improving your English before you take IELTS.	you may get an acceptable score under examination conditions but we recommend that you think about having more practice or lessons before you take IELTS.	you are likely to get an acceptable score under examination conditions but remember that different institutions will find different scores acceptable.

TEST 3

LISTENING

 Answer key with extra explanations in Resource bank

Part 1, Questions 1–10

1 furniture
2 meetings
3 diary
4 detail(s)
5 1 / one year
6 deliveries
7 tidy
8 team
9 heavy
10 customer

Part 2, Questions 11–20

11 B
12 A
13 C
14 B
15 C
16 B
17&18 *IN EITHER ORDER*
    B
    D
19&20 *IN EITHER ORDER*
    A
    E

Part 3, Questions 21–30

21 page
22 size
23 graphic(s)
24 structure
25 purpose
26 assumption(s)
27 A
28 C
29 C
30 B

Part 4, Questions 31–40

31 mud
32 clay
33 metal
34 hair
35 bath(s)
36 disease(s)
37 perfume
38 salt
39 science
40 tax

If you score ...

0–17	18–27	28–40
you are unlikely to get an acceptable score under examination conditions and we recommend that you spend a lot of time improving your English before you take IELTS.	you may get an acceptable score under examination conditions but we recommend that you think about having more practice or lessons before you take IELTS.	you are likely to get an acceptable score under examination conditions but remember that different institutions will find different scores acceptable.

TEST 3

READING

 Answer key with extra explanations in Resource bank

Reading Passage 1, Questions 1–13

1 TRUE
2 FALSE
3 NOT GIVEN
4 TRUE
5 NOT GIVEN
6 FALSE
7 TRUE
8 resignation
9 materials
10 miners
11 family
12 collectors
13 income

Reading Passage 2, Questions 14–26

14 iii
15 vi
16 v
17 x
18 iv
19 viii
20 i

21 wheels
22 film
23 filter
24 waste
25 performance
26 servicing

Reading Passage 3, Questions 27–40

27 C
28 B
29 F
30 A
31 E
32 D
33 F
34 B
35 C
36 G
37 B
38 D
39 A
40 A

If you score ...

0–16	17–25	26–40
you are unlikely to get an acceptable score under examination conditions and we recommend that you spend a lot of time improving your English before you take IELTS.	you may get an acceptable score under examination conditions but we recommend that you think about having more practice or lessons before you take IELTS.	you are likely to get an acceptable score under examination conditions but remember that different institutions will find different scores acceptable.

TEST 4

LISTENING

 Answer key with extra explanations in Resource bank

Part 1, Questions 1–10

1 journalist
2 shopping
3 Staunfirth
4 return
5 23.70
6 online
7 delay
8 information
9 platform(s)
10 parking

Part 3, Questions 21–30

21 B
22 A
23 B
24 A
25 A
26 A
27 B
28 B
29 A
30 C

Part 2, Questions 11–20

11 D
12 C
13 G
14 H
15 A
16 E
17&18 *IN EITHER ORDER*
    A
    D
19&20 *IN EITHER ORDER*
    A
    C

Part 4, Questions 31–40

31 wealth
32 technology
33 power
34 textile(s)
35 machines
36 newspapers
37 local
38 lighting
39 windows
40 Advertising

If you score ...

0–18	19–27	28–40
you are unlikely to get an acceptable score under examination conditions and we recommend that you spend a lot of time improving your English before you take IELTS.	you may get an acceptable score under examination conditions but we recommend that you think about having more practice or lessons before you take IELTS.	you are likely to get an acceptable score under examination conditions but remember that different institutions will find different scores acceptable.

TEST 4

READING

 Answer key with extra explanations in Resource bank

Reading Passage 1,
Questions 1–13

1 water
2 diet
3 drought
4 erosion
5 desert
6 (its / huarango / the) branches
7 *IN EITHER ORDER (BOTH REQUIRED FOR ONE MARK)*
  leaves (and)
  bark
8 (its / huarango / the) trunk
9 NOT GIVEN
10 FALSE
11 TRUE
12 FALSE
13 NOT GIVEN

Reading Passage 2,
Questions 14–26

14 NOT GIVEN
15 FALSE
16 TRUE
17 FALSE
18 FALSE
19 TRUE

20 words
21 finger
22 direction
23 commands
24 fires
25 technology
26 award

Reading Passage 3,
Questions 27–40

27 D
28 E
29 F
30 H
31 B
32 C
33 D
34 B
35 YES
36 NOT GIVEN
37 NO
38 YES
39 NOT GIVEN
40 D

If you score …

0–16	17–25	26–40
you are unlikely to get an acceptable score under examination conditions and we recommend that you spend a lot of time improving your English before you take IELTS.	you may get an acceptable score under examination conditions but we recommend that you think about having more practice or lessons before you take IELTS.	you are likely to get an acceptable score under examination conditions but remember that different institutions will find different scores acceptable.

Sample Writing answers

 Additional sample Writing answers in Resource bank

TEST 1, WRITING TASK 1

This is an answer written by a candidate who achieved a **Band 6.0** score.

The table depicts the outcomes of a questionare of how often people buy and drink a different types of coffee in Sydney, Melbourne, Brisbane, Adelaide, and Hobart of Australia.

The first option is bought fresh coffee in last 4 weeks. In Sydney has 43.7 per cent of city residents and has almost the same amount as Melbourne which is 42.2 per cent. Brisbane and Adelaide have a nearly same amount, 34.2 per cent and 34.4 per cent. Next, Hobart has 38.3 per cent.

The second line is bought instant coffee in last 4 weeks. Brisbane has 52.6 per cent. Other two cities that have amost the same number are Adelaide, 49.8 per cent, and Melbourne, 48.3 per cent. The lowest number is 45.5 per cent of Sydney and The highest number is 54.1 per cent of Hobart.

The last option of the survey shows the percentage of city residents that went to a cafe' for coffee or tea in last 4 weeks. In Sydney, people went to a cafe' for coffee or tea in last 4 weeks 61 per cent of city residents. In Brisbane, citizens went to a cafe' for coffee of tea in last 4 weeks 55.4 per cent. The lowest is Adelaide that shows 49.9 per cent of city residents. In Hobart, people went to a cafe' for coffee of tea in last 4 weeks 62.7 per cent. The highest is Melbourne that shows 63.3 per cent.

In conclusion, the highest number of the survey is the percentage of city residents that went to a cafe for coffee or tea in last 4 weeks because it shows almost the highest percentage in 3 types.

Here is the examiner's comment:

> This answer covers all three categories and shows a good level of grouping and comparison of information in each category. The descriptions are supported by accurate data. Organisation is clear (introduction and overview, one paragraph per category) and there is evidence of cohesive devices [*The first option* | *The second line* | *The last option*]. Vocabulary is generally adequate and appropriate for the task, in spite of occasional errors [*questionare* / questionnaire | *amost* / almost]. Grammar shows a mix of simple and complex sentence structures with a reasonable level of accuracy. A wider range of vocabulary and/or grammatical range would help to improve the score here.

TEST 1, WRITING TASK 2

This is an answer written by a candidate who achieved a **Band 7.0** score.

In some countries the ownership of peoples' home is an important matter. In these countries it is very important to own your own home rather than renting it. It might be indifferent for some, but for these people it matter.

Why is that the case? you might wonder. I think it is because your home is supposed to be exactly what it sounds like, your home. As a human I think we long after having stuff to call our own, doesn't matter what it is, but humans will always want to claim ownership. This is nothing new and it has been like this through human history, like colonies for example, which later once again became the same country as before lead by its own inhabitants. People will always want to be the one to decide what happens to them and when you rent your home you can't even paint it without the owners permission.

If you as a person are renting an apartment there might be a lot of stressors in your life. A scratched wall can cause you a major headache, because the wall was not yours. The bedroom you are currently sleeping in might not be available as long as you hope, things happen in life and maybe the next landlord won't want to have you as a tenant.

In other perspective, not owning your home could be a relief when it comes to your finance. As a renter you won't have to pay mortgage, take loans or spend an awful lot of money on buying the property. You wouldn't have to worry about the house market crashing or a natural disaster destroying your expensive home.

Bottom line, as a human I feel like we need to have a home and calling it your own can make that more special. I personally would rather own my house, because then whatever happens it is on me and no one else.

Here is the examiner's comment:

> The candidate clearly explains why home ownership may be of importance to some people. She or he also explores the positive and negative sides of owning your own home before putting forward his or her own opinion. The task is well addressed and ideas are explored in some depth. Organisation is clear, with good use of cohesive devices and paragraphing and the message is easy to follow. The range of vocabulary is appropriate, with examples of less common items [*long after* / for | *house* / housing *market*] and good use of collocations [*claim ownership* | *a major headache* | *pay mortgage* | *natural disaster* | The *bottom line*]. There is a variety of complex sentence structures, with a high level of accuracy and only a minor error in punctuation [*owners* / owner's].

TEST 2, WRITING TASK 1

This is an answer written by a candidate who achieved a **Band 7.0** score.

The graph displays the statistics of (the number at tourists visiting a particular carribean island between (the years) 2010 and 2017) in the year 2010, there were a quarter of a million visitors that stayed on cruise ships, while another 750000 visitors were staying on island that totals up to a million of visitors during that year. The following year, which is 2011, half a million visitors stayed on cruise ships for the visitors who were staying on the island, the graph doesn't show and decrease or an increase because the number was the same as the previous year, which is 750000 visitors. Total visitors for that year was 1 million and a quarter visitors. Moving on, the number of visitors staying on cruise ships decreased to 250000 visitors in the year 2012 while the number of visitors staying on island increased to 1250000 people. This sums up to an amount of 1500000 visitors that year.

In the year 2013, 500000 visitors stayed on cruise ships while 1500000 visitors stayed on island that adds up to 2 million visitors that year. During the next year which is 2014, a total at one million visitors stayed on cruise ships while the same number of visitors staying on island remained consistent which is 1500000 people, totalling up to two million and a half visitors that year. For the year 2015, 1250000 visitors were staying on cruise ships and 1500000 tourists were staying on island, showing no changes from the previous year. The total of tourists in that year increased to 2750000 visitors. The total number of visitors remained the same in the following year which is 2016 where it summed up 1500000 visitors staying on cruise ships and 1250000 visitors staying on island. In the final year. 2017, the number of visitors staying on cruise ships and staying on island increase to three and a half million of visitors. The graph showed an increase of half a million for the number of visitors staying on cruise ships which totals up to two million visitors. As for the number of visitors staying on island, the graph also increased for a quarter million which adds up to a total of 1500000 visitors that year.

Through the years, the number of visitors staying on cruise ships showed an unstable increase and decrease for the first four years, but continued to increase in the next year onwards. As for the number of visitors staying on island, there was no progress of increase or decrease in the first two years which are 2010 and 2011 but the graph rose until it remained constant for three consecutive years in a row. The number of visitors then slacked off in the year 2016, but managed to increase to the same level as the year before the previous in 2017. All in all, the graph showed an outstanding performance for the total number of visitors throughout 2011 to 2017, where it increased gradually every single year except from 2015 to 2016 where it remained constant.

Here is the examiner's comment:

> This is a full and detailed description of the data contained in the graph, supplemented by a comparison of the variations in the numbers for the two types of visitors (staying on cruise ships or staying on the island). There is a clear overview at the end of the description. Organisation is fairly clear and progresses logically across the time period, although it could be improved by subdividing the rather long second paragraph. The range of vocabulary is wide enough to show some variety of expression [*adds up to* | *totals up to*] and some use of collocation [*three … years in a row*]. There is a high level of accuracy in grammatical control, in both simple and complex structures, but there is an omission of a full stop between the first and second sentences and no capital letter to indicate the beginning of the new sentence.

TEST 2, WRITING TASK 2

This is an answer written by a candidate who achieved a **Band 6.0** score.

Todays technologies enable us to read book on electronic devices and what's more, we can store hundreds of thousands of books on devices like Amazon's kindle e-reader. This makes some people to believe that people will stop printing books and in the future, everything will be digitalized.

Electronic books and newspapers have many advantages. They are easy to use and rech. They can be stored in computers, mobiles, e-readers and in cloud in huge amounts and are available at any time. The cost of manufacturing and printing is completely removed, which reduced their price. Digital book and newspapers also have one very important advantage – they are environmentally friendly. No paper is used to print magazines and books, which means less trees are cut from our forests to produce papers. All of these factors convinced many people that digital versions of books and magazines is more convenient, ethical and cheaper choice.

On the other hand, traditional printed books and magazines have existed for centuries and I believe they have created some kind of emotional connection and value for people. When a man reads a book and he likes it, he most probably would like to have it in a form of a tangible thing. Books are a form of art, like statues and paintings. You can have a picture of some famous painting, but the painting itself has some intangible value. Magazines and newspapers do not have such a value in themselves.

Based on this, I believe that the amount of books are printed will decrease considerably and maybe even dramatically, however printed, tangible books will still be demanded by many people as they have some aura and value in addition to the things that are written inside.

I do think, though, that there is a big chance magazines and newspapers will move into the online world completely. This is because they are published in huge numbers daily and weekly and monthly and no one needs them after years. Printing so huge amount of articles will demand additional recources and make them less competitive even in terms of price.

Sample Writing answers

Here is the examiner's comment:

This is a thoughtful exploration of the topic. The writer considers the advantages of having online materials rather than printed ones, and also examines why printed books may not totally disappear, although other printed materials, such as magazines and newspapers, may become completely digitalised. The score might be improved by further exploration of whether online materials will be free, as cost is mentioned only briefly. Organisation is clear, paragraphing is logical and linking words and phrases guide the reader through the script [*All of these factors* | *On the other hand* | *Based on this*]. The range of vocabulary is quite varied, with many examples of collocation [*electronic devices* | *Digital book and newspapers* | *environmentally friendly* | *digital versions* | *traditional printed books* | *emotional connection and value*] with only two spelling errors [*rech* / reach | *recources* / resources]. There is a mix of simple and complex sentence structures and these are generally accurate. Some errors do occur [*Todays* / Today's | *to read book*(s) | *makes some people to believe* / makes some people believe | *digital versions of books … is* / are *more convenient* | *Printing so* / such a *huge amount of articles*], but the meaning is still clear.

TEST 3, WRITING TASK 1

This is an answer written by a candidate who achieved a **Band 6.5** score.

The given scheme explains the process of instant noodles production. Moreover it reveals how this product appears on super market shelves. In general, there are eight stages of manufacturing before the final product is being delivered to the store.

The first operation consists of putting flour into storage silos. Then the flour is mixed with some other ingredients into dough in a special machine. The substance is further stretched into sheets which a cut into thin strips during the fourth stage. The following operation involves the strips too. At this moment the noodles are formed into discs. After that the round-shaped figures are cooked in oil and dried. The seventh stage consists of placing the product into cups and adding some vegetables and spices to it. The final part of production process is mainly about the packaging. At this moment freshly printed lables are added to the cups which are sealed after that. As soon as the product (instant noodles) is ready to leave the factory, it is shipped to a shopping facility.

Overall, it takes a considerably long time for a product to get to a super market.

Here is the examiner's comment:

> This response addresses the task fully and provides a description for each stage of the process, along with supporting details. A stronger overview would help to raise the overall score. Information is logically organised and the reader is guided through the answer by a range of cohesive devices [*Moreover* | *In general* | *The first operation* | *Then* | *further* | *too* | *At this moment* | *After that* | *The seventh stage* | *The final part* | *Overall*]. There is also use of reference [*this*] and substitution [*product*] to add variety to the description. There is some flexibility in the use of vocabulary [Labelling + sealing → *lables* / labels *are added to the cups which are sealed*] and there is good use of less common items [*The substance* | *round-shaped figures* | *the product* | *packaging*]. There is a variety of complex structures used and most of these are accurate: there is an error in line 6 [*which a cut* / which are cut].

TEST 3, WRITING TASK 2

This is an answer written by a candidate who achieved a **Band 7.0** score.

Advertisement has always been a crucial part in the world of marketing. Throughout the decade, we have seen a significant increase in the amount of advertisements, whether it is on the media like television or widespread through social network platforms. The goal of advertisements is to get consumers to buy a targeted product, and while this method has been proven considerably successful generally, some people view it as too prevalent to catch the consumers' attention any more.

Advertisements can act as a strong persuasion device to seemingly hypnotize people into buying goods and services. This is so because of the tactics placed in the messages, such as showing people having a good time together when using a particular product, using bandwagen, showing only the upsides of usage, and applying compare and contrast strategies to show the effects of using the product and make it stand out. Even if people do not know it, these messages are repeated several times and soon it may brainwash people to Finally go out and get the product. For instance, if a person is watching television and sees a certain advertisement of a snack many times, the repeated sight of the scrumptious food may result in that person feeling hungry and succumbing to the advertisement at last.

Nevertheless, there is another point of view in which the widespread of advertisements makes it a normal thing. After watching a dozen of advertisements people will see it as a mere every day routine and cease to pay attention to the message of the advertisement. Some people may even choose to turn off a television channel, for instance, only just to avoid seeing and hearing repetetive advertisements. After a certain frequency, they start to get bored and stop paying attention to ads. Hence, in the end, the main goal of advertisements is not complete since the people whom the messages are sent out to do not receive that message. A real life example can be seen from advertisements in a particular social media platform, Youtube. In the Youtube marketing mechanism, advertisements are place before and in between videos, hoping that the viewers would also be forced to watch the advertisements, too. However, this is not usually the case, since many people would just click "Skip Ad" and continue on.

In conclusion, advertisements can be successful in persuading people to purchase goods and services, or they can be unsuccessful in many ways. They are very commonly seen nowadays, but not all of them fulfill their purpose. Thus, advertisements must be designed and presented in the correct way to result in the highest effectiveness.

Here is the examiner's comment:

> This candidate has addressed all parts of the prompt and presents a clear position throughout the response. Main ideas are presented, extended and supported. Ideas and information are presented logically and there is a clear progression throughout the answer. There is a range of cohesive devices [*For instance* | *Nevertheless* | *Hence* | *A real life example* | *However* | *In conclusion* | *Thus*], including reference and substitution [*this method* | *this is so* | *these messages*]. The range of vocabulary is wide enough to show some precise meanings and also shows less common items [*prevalent* | *hypnotize* | *tactics* | *brainwash* | *succumbing*] and collocations [*significant increase* | *catch the consumers' attention* | *having a good time together* | *compare and contrast strategies*]. There are only occasional spelling errors [*bandwagen* / bandwagon | *repetetive* / repetitive]. There is a variety of complex structures and the writer shows good control over grammar and punctuation.

TEST 4, WRITING TASK 1

This is an answer written by a candidate who achieved a **Band 6.0** score.

The chart demonstrates what Anthropology graduates from one university did after finishing their undergraduate degree course. The table indicates the salaries of the anthropologists in work after 5 years.

As we can see from the pie chart, majority of Anthropology graduates are employed. Fifty-two per cent of them have a full-time job. Almost twenty per cent of graduates have either a part-time work or it is combined with post grad study. Eight per cent of students continue their full-time education. Only twelve per cent of graduates are unemployed. The information about all the rest graduates is unknown.

Thus, most of Anthropology graduates have a job. Half of those who work in Government sector earn more than a hundred thousand dollars. It is less than proportion of freelance concultantants who get the same amount of money. Besides, it is only one-third of those who work for private companies. We can see nearly the same percentage of those who get from fifty thousand dollars to ninty-nine thousand dollars as freelance consultants and in government sector. The situation is different in private companies. More of them get from fifty thousand to seventy-four thousand dollars than from seventy-five to ninety-nine thousand dollars. The proportion of those who work for private companies for from twenty-five thousand to forty-nine thousand dollars is half bigger than the same one in government sector and as freelancers.

So, the chart and the table show us that most of Anthropology graduates are employed and a salary more than twenty-five thousand dollars after five year's work.

Here is the examiner's comment:

> The candidate has described all the key features and has supported these with relevant figures. There is some comparison of the figures in both the chart and the table. Information is presented coherently and there is a clear overall progression (introduction, description of the pie chart information, description of the information in the table and conclusion). Some cohesive devices are used to organise the description [*As we can see* | *Thus* | *Besides* | *So*]. The range of vocabulary is adequate for the task [*combined with* | *earn* | *proportion of* | *freelancers*], but there are some errors [*all the rest graduates* / all the rest of the graduates | *It is less* / more than (the) proportion of freelance … same amount of money | *concultantants* / consultants | *ninty* / ninety | *half bigger than* / twice as big as]. There is a mix of simple and complex sentence structures, with some errors [(the) *majority* | ~~a~~ *part-time work* | *all the rest* (of the) *graduates* | *in* (the) *Government sector*].

TEST 4, WRITING TASK 2

This is an answer written by a candidate who achieved a **Band 6.5** score.

Is it right to tell children they can achieve anything by trying hard?

In some cultures, children are often told that they can achieve anything if they try hard enough. Giving this message to them can produce several effects on each child.

In the social point of view, telling this to children is very important because we are motivating the child not to give up. We are making him to try hard, to make an effort, to read between lines and at the end of that long path achieve their objectives. Telling that they can achieve anything if they try hard enough, we are saying in other words that things are not so simple or easy but they are not imposible, is all about working hard and doing our best.

Sometimes this is not helpfull because we not always achieve our dreams or goals but it does not mean we did not try hard, it was just because another person deserve it more than us. So, although we try hard, there are other factors playing a role in our path.

In the economic point of view, if our objectives demand a lot of money, we are again in the same situation, although we work hard, it would be difficult to achieve it.

To sum up, we are teaching to children how life works, it demands hard work, effort, dedication, time doing things we don't like, studying and attitude. And at the end, if you have done all these things but you still did not achieve your goal, you will be happy anyway because you did your best.

Here is the examiner's comment:

> This candidate has presented some ideas on both sides of the topic, though there is room for further development. Ideas are logically organised and there is a clear progression throughout. Cohesive devices, including reference and substitution, are generally well managed [*this message* | *In* / From *the social point of view* | *telling this to children* | *the same situation* | *To sum up*]. The range of vocabulary is wide enough to show some variety, some less common items and collocations [*motivating* | *give up* | *try hard* | *make an effort* | *achieve their objectives* | *dedication*] and there are few spelling errors. There is a mix of simple and complex sentence structures, some of which are accurate [*we are saying … that things are not so … easy but they are not imposible* | *we are teaching … children how life works* | *if you have done all these things but you still did not achieve your goal, you will be happy anyway because you did your best*]. Others contain errors [*making him to try hard* / making him try hard | *is all about working hard* / it is all about working hard |
> *we not always achieve* / we do not always achieve | *another person deserve* / another person deserved], but the meaning is still clear.

Sample answer sheets

BRITISH COUNCIL **idp** **Cambridge Assessment English**

IELTS Listening Answer Sheet

Candidate Name

Candidate No.

Centre No.

Test Date   Day   Month   Year

Listening Listening Listening Listening Listening Listening Listening

Marker use only

1		21	
2		22	
3		23	
4		24	
5		25	
6		26	
7		27	
8		28	
9		29	
10		30	
11		31	
12		32	
13		33	
14		34	
15		35	
16		36	
17		37	
18		38	
19		39	
20		40	

Marker 2 Signature:

Marker 1 Signature:

Listening Total:

20656

© Cambridge Assessment 2020   Photocopiable

BRITISH COUNCIL   **idp**   **Cambridge Assessment English**

IELTS Reading Answer Sheet

Candidate Name

Candidate No.

Centre No.

Test Module   ☐ Academic   ☐ General Training

Test Date   Day   Month   Year

Reading Reading Reading Reading Reading Reading Reading

Marker use only

1		1 ✓ ✗
2		2 ✓ ✗
3		3 ✓ ✗
4		4 ✓ ✗
5		5 ✓ ✗
6		6 ✓ ✗
7		7 ✓ ✗
8		8 ✓ ✗
9		9 ✓ ✗
10		10 ✓ ✗
11		11 ✓ ✗
12		12 ✓ ✗
13		13 ✓ ✗
14		14 ✓ ✗
15		15 ✓ ✗
16		16 ✓ ✗
17		17 ✓ ✗
18		18 ✓ ✗
19		19 ✓ ✗
20		20 ✓ ✗

Marker use only

21		21 ✓ ✗
22		22 ✓ ✗
23		23 ✓ ✗
24		24 ✓ ✗
25		25 ✓ ✗
26		26 ✓ ✗
27		27 ✓ ✗
28		28 ✓ ✗
29		29 ✓ ✗
30		30 ✓ ✗
31		31 ✓ ✗
32		32 ✓ ✗
33		33 ✓ ✗
34		34 ✓ ✗
35		35 ✓ ✗
36		36 ✓ ✗
37		37 ✓ ✗
38		38 ✓ ✗
39		39 ✓ ✗
40		40 ✓ ✗

Marker 2 Signature:

Marker 1 Signature:

Reading Total:

61788

BRITISH COUNCIL

idp

Cambridge Assessment English

IELTS Writing Answer Sheet - TASK 1

Candidate Name

Candidate No.

Centre No.

Test Module ☐ Academic ☐ General Training

Test Date Day Month Year

If you need more space to write your answer, use an additional sheet and write in the space provided to indicate how many sheets you are using: Sheet of

Writing Task 1 Writing Task 1 Writing Task 1 Writing Task 1

Do not write below this line

Do not write in this area. Please continue your answer on the other side of this sheet.

23505

BRITISH COUNCIL **idp** **Cambridge Assessment English**

IELTS Writing Answer Sheet - TASK 2

Candidate Name

Candidate No. Centre No.

Test Module ☐ Academic ☐ General Training Test Date Day Month Year

If you need more space to write your answer, use an additional sheet and write in the space provided to indicate how many sheets you are using: Sheet of

Writing Task 2 Writing Task 2 Writing Task 2 Writing Task 2

Do not write below this line

Do not write in this area. Please continue your answer on the other side of this sheet.

39507

Acknowledgements

The authors and publishers acknowledge the following sources of copyright material and are grateful for the permissions granted. While every effort has been made, it has not always been possible to identify the sources of all the material used, or to trace all copyright holders. If any omissions are brought to our notice, we will be happy to include the appropriate acknowledgements on reprinting and in the next update to the digital edition, as applicable.

Text

Reading – Test 1: NewStatesman for the adapted text from 'Driverless cars shift up a gear' by Professor Nick Reed, *NewStatesman*, 06.05.2016. Copyright © NewStatesman. Reproduced with permission; An extract of text from *The Faber Book of Exploration* by Benedict Allen. Copyright © Benedict Allen. Reproduced with kind permission; Roy Morgan Research for the adapted text from 'Caffeine wars: which city is Australia's coffee capital?', 24.03.2015. https://www.foodprocessing.com.au/content/business-solutions/news/is-sydney-the-real-coffee-capital-of-australia–965774561. Copyright © Roy Morgan Research. Reproduced with kind permission; **Test 2**: Theatrum Mundi for the adapted text from 'Engineers could learn a lot from dance when designing urban transport' by John Bingham-Hall. Copyright © 2017 John Bingham-Hall. Reproduced with permission; Syon Geographical Ltd for the adapted text from 'Back to life: the world of de-extinction' by Chris Fitch, *Geographical Magazine*, 17.02.2017. Copyright © 2017 Syon Geographical Ltd. Reproduced with permission; APS observer by AMERICAN PSYCHOLOGICAL SOCIETY. Republished with permission of Association for Psychological Science from 'The Science of Humor Is No Laughing Matter' by Alexandra Michel, 2017; permission conveyed through Copyright Clearance Center, Inc. **Test 3**: Encyclopædia Britannica for the adapted text with permission from the *Encyclopædia Britannica*, © 2019 by Encyclopædia Britannica, Inc. Reproduced with permission; *The Guardian* for the adapted text from 'The innovators: desalination unit brings clean water on wheels' by Shane Hickey, *The Guardian*, 01.07.2016. Copyright Guardian News & Media Ltd 2019. Reproduced with permission; New Scientist Ltd for the adapted text from 'Why fairy tales are really scary tales' by Penny Sarchet, *New Scientist Ltd*, 15.12.2015. Copyright © 2017 New Scientist Ltd. All rights reserved. Distributed by Tribune Content Agency. Reproduced with permission; Maruchan Inc. for the adapted diagram of 'Manufacturing instant noodles' by Maruchan Inc. Copyright © Maruchan Inc. Reproduced with kind permission; **Test 4**: Syon Geographical Ltd for the adapted text from 'The return of the huarango' by Olivia Edward, *Geographical Magazine*. Copyright © 2010 Syon Geographical Ltd. Reproduced with permission; *National Geographic* for the adapted text from 'Hey Luis, Don't Forget Tomatoes, She Whistled' by Marilyn Terrell, *National Geographic Society*. Copyright © 2015–2019 National Geographic Partners, LLC. All rights reserved. Reproduced with permission.

Listening – Harper Collins Publishers Ltd for the adapted text *Consuming passions* by Judith Flanders. Reprinted by permission of HarperCollins Publishers Ltd. Copyright © 2006 Judith Flanders. Reproduced with kind permission; Rogers, Coleridge and White for the adapted text *Consuming passions* by Judith Flanders. Copyright © 2013 Rogers, Coleridge and White; AM Heath & Co. Ltd for the adapted text *Consuming Passions* by Judith Flanders. Copyright © 2008 Judith Flanders. Reproduced by permission of AM Heath & Co. Ltd; Excerpt(s) from *Collapse: How Societies Choose to Fail or Succeed* by Jared Diamond, copyright © 2005 by Jared Diamond. Used by permission of Viking Books, an imprint of Penguin Publishing Group, a division of Penguin Random House LLC. All rights reserved; Seven hundred and ninety-one (791) words in the English language from *Collapse* by Jared Diamond Copyright © Jared Diamond, 2005, 2011.

Illustration

Illustrations commissioned by Cambridge Assessment.

Audio

Audio production by Real Deal Productions and dsound recording.

Typesetting

Typeset by QBS Learning.

URLs

The publisher has used its best endeavours to ensure that the URLs for external websites referred to in this book are correct and active at the time of going to press. However, the publisher has no responsibility for the websites and can make no guarantee that a site will remain live or that the content is or will remain appropriate.

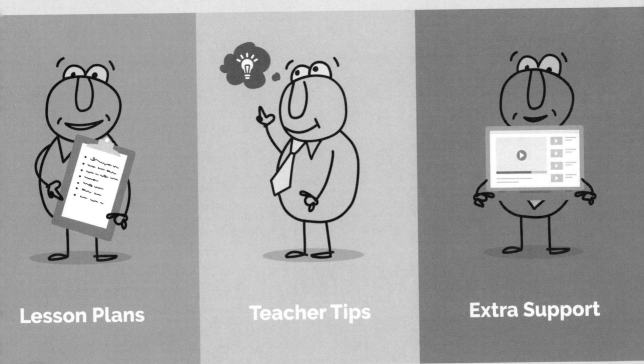

PRACTICE TESTS EXACTLY LIKE THE REAL THING!

9781316637869

9781316637876

Cambridge English IELTS 13 ACADEMIC WITH ANSWERS AUTHENTIC EXAMINATION PAPERS

9781108553094

9781108553193

9781108681315

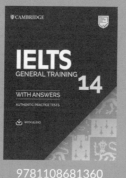

9781108681360

PREPARATION MATERIALS YOU CAN TRUST

9780521692465

9780521604628

9780521709750

9781107620698

Buy online or from your local bookstore